GEORGE BALANCHINE

Eminent Lives, brief biographies by distinguished authors on canonical figures, joins a long tradition in this lively form, from Plutarch's *Lives* to Vasari's *Lives of the Painters,* Dr. Johnson's *Lives of the Poets* to Lytton Strachey's *Eminent Victorians.* Pairing great subjects with writers known for their strong sensibilities and sharp, lively points of view, the Eminent Lives are ideal introductions designed to appeal to the general reader, the student, and the scholar. "To preserve a becoming brevity which excludes everything that is redundant and nothing that is significant," wrote Strachey: "That, surely, is the first duty of the biographer."

GEORGE BALANCHINE

The Ballet Maker

Robert Gottlieb

EMINENT LIVES

ATLAS
BOOKS

HarperCollins*Publishers*

For Barbara Horgan,

not because of all she's done for me,

but because of all she's done for Balanchine

GEORGE BALANCHINE. Copyright © 2004 by Robert Gottlieb. All rights
reserved. Printed in the United States of America. No part of this book may
be used or reproduced in any manner whatsoever without written permission
except in the case of brief quotations embodied in critical articles and reviews.
For information, address HarperCollins Publishers Inc., 10 East 53rd Street,
New York, NY 10022.

HarperCollins books may be purchased for educational, business, or sales
promotional use. For information, please write: Special Markets Department,
HarperCollins Publishers Inc., 10 East 53rd Street, New York, NY 10022.

FIRST EDITION

Designed by Elliott Beard and Amy Hill

Printed on acid-free paper

Library of Congress Cataloging-in-Publication Data
Gottlieb, Robert.
    George Balanchine : the ballet maker / Robert Gottlieb.—1st ed.
        p. cm.—(Eminent lives)
    Includes bibiliographical references.
    ISBN 0-06-075070-7
    1. Balanchine, George. 2. Choreographers—United States—Biography.
    I. Title. II. Series.
GV1785.B32G68 2004
792.8'2'092—dc22   2004048856
[B]

04   05   06   07   08   ❖/RRD   10   9   8   7   6   5   4   3   2   1

Contents

A Personal Note   *1*

CHAPTER 1: *In Russia*   *7*

CHAPTER 2: *With Diaghilev*   *29*

CHAPTER 3: *On His Own*   *55*

CHAPTER 4: *To America*   *73*

CHAPTER 5: *Broadway and Hollywood*   *87*

CHAPTER 6: *His Women and His Men*   *115*

CHAPTER 7: *The New York City Ballet*   *147*

CHAPTER 8: *Back to Russia*   *163*

CHAPTER 9: *The Final Years*   *175*

CHAPTER 10: *The Man*   *185*

Words by George Balanchine   *199*
Significant Balanchine Works   *207*
Sources   *209*
Acknowledgments   *215*

A Personal Note

George Balanchine's centenary year, 2004, seemed to me the appropriate moment to publish a compact biography of him. Unlike so many other artists dominant in their day, he has not receded into history since his death. Rather, in the past twenty-one years his influence has become more pervasive than ever as his ballets spread throughout the world, sometimes dominating, always enhancing the repertories they enter. And now that we can step back and consider his life as a whole with some historical perspective, the trajectory of that life and the richness of his achievement invite new examination and celebration.

I first encountered Balanchine's work in 1948, my last year of high school, when one of my teachers, for reasons known only to herself, took a friend and me to a performance of Ballet Society at New York's City Center. I didn't know why I was there, but I knew that I loved what I saw. That fall, Ballet Society morphed into New York City Ballet, and since I was by then a freshman at Columbia, and the prices at the City Center were extremely low,

I was able to follow the first four years of the company very closely. These were the years of *Orpheus, Symphony in C,* and *Bourrée Fantasque*; of *The Four Temperaments, Concerto Barocco,* and *La Valse*; of Maria Tallchief and Tanaquil LeClercq, Jerome Robbins and Nora Kaye and Melissa Hayden, Nicholas Magallanes and Francisco Moncion and André Eglevsky. At the time I knew very little about ballet; I only knew how elated I felt every time I watched Balanchine.

As the years—the decades—went by, and as Balanchine kept producing miracles of invention, I began to grasp the scope and depth of his genius. Eventually, as I grew more aware of ballet's history, I came to understand his unique place in it. With his roots in the classicism of Petipa and the nineteenth-century Russian tradition, his grasp of the French Opéra ballet style, his profound understanding of ballet pedagogy, his absorption of popular dance influences from the waltz to the hornpipe to jazz to Astaire to square dance, his education by Stravinsky and Diaghilev in neoclassicism, his fearless extensions (but never betrayals) of classical technique, his genius for telling a story, his overwhelmingly sensitive response to music, he carried within him all of ballet, past and present, and was constantly redefining its future. Looking backward and looking forward were not separate matters for him; he summed up everything even as he was reinventing everything.

Like comparable geniuses in other art forms—Shakespeare, Mozart—he composed with amazing fluency and ease; works poured from him without apparent hitch or hesitation. From the

very beginning of his career, between the desire and the act fell no shadow. He didn't wait for divine inspiration—when there was something to be done, he just got to work. Always he adjusted himself to the immediate situation, whatever it was: big stage or little stage; large cast or small; money or no money; ballet, musical comedy, film, or television. And he was always fast, and practical: Situations were there to be exploited, problems were there to be solved. He was a leader, a model—both a supreme artist and a brilliant executive. To his dancers he was everything. To other choreographers he was a figure of awe. As Twyla Tharp has put it, "Balanchine is God."

I came to know him and work with him through Lincoln Kirstein, the man who brought him to America. In the early seventies, I edited several of Kirstein's books, beginning with *The New York City Ballet,* and Kirstein invited me to join a new board of directors he was assembling for that company. At first I demurred, on the grounds that I wasn't good with rich people and couldn't raise money. He assured me that he needed me there only because "I want someone on the board who knows ballet and will understand what to do at the critical moment"— the critical moment, I realized, being the one when Balanchine would have to be replaced. In fact, there was no real crisis when that moment came, many years later. But long before then, I had begun performing a number of tasks for the company, whose management level was overstretched. Having learned what I could from the three people in charge—Betty Cage, Eddie Bigelow, and Barbara Horgan—I was soon programming the

ballet seasons and overseeing their marketing from my office, first at Alfred Knopf, then at *The New Yorker*. I was also involved with labor negotiations and pricing decisions, occasionally acting as company spokesman, and often traveling with the company.

Through those years I spent a considerable amount of time with Balanchine, since there were always issues to discuss. Sometimes I would stand with him in the wings watching performances, sometimes I would go to his office, and in a real crisis I would call him at home. He was always calm, always courteous, always realistic, and always impersonal. I never tried to develop a personal relationship with him—there was no need for one, and I had no wish for one. To me, too, he was a god, and I saw my role as being some kind of messenger of the gods. In fact, I couldn't understand why he was permitting an outsider from another world, whom he hardly knew, to undertake these responsibilities. When, early on, I asked Barbara Horgan, his personal assistant, why he accepted me to the extent that he was even aware of my existence, she explained that my name—"Gottlieb"—was the German equivalent of "Amadeus," and that the Mozart connection was good enough for him.

My impressions of Balanchine, then, come from close contact but don't reflect the slightest touch of intimacy or even of friendship. Also, of course, I was observing him only in the last dozen years of his life. But it was a great privilege to have known him at all, and an even greater one to have been able to serve him, in however limited a way. The greatest privilege was one I shared

with many others: living, from season to season, through the thirty-five years of his engagement with his City Ballet dancers. It wasn't simply a matter of enjoying a number of wonderful performances. For people like me, the New York City Ballet, as Arlene Croce once put it, has been "our civilization."

The Family

Top: George's father and mother, Mcliton and Maria Balanchivadze

Left: George, Andrei, and Tamara

Right: Andrei, Tamara, and George

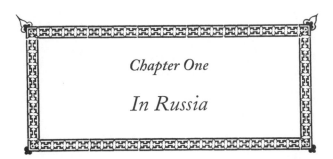

Chapter One

In Russia

George Balanchine was born in St. Petersburg in 1904, the year after Marius Petipa (*The Sleeping Beauty*) created his last ballet at the Maryinsky Imperial Theatre and the year before Michel Fokine (*Les Sylphides*) created his first. It was the year in which Isadora Duncan made her first appearance in Russia, encouraging Fokine and others in their impulse toward change. And within the next five years the Russian exodus to the West had begun: Pavlova to her eternal touring, Diaghilev with his Ballets Russes to Paris, with Nijinsky and Karsavina in tow. Dancers in St. Petersburg were asserting their views and demanding new rights, which led to a crackdown by management. Russian ballet, on a more or less even keel for decades (apart from the usual internecine conflicts), was in turmoil, and the conservatives chose to consider these disturbing phenomena as hotheaded rebellion rather than as necessary correctives.

The political situation was, of course, equally incendiary. On Balanchine's first birthday, January 22, 1905, a group of protesting workers with their families were fired upon in St. Petersburg,

and many of them were killed. The slide toward World War I, revolution, and communism had begun.

The immediate world Balanchine was born into, however, was not caught up directly either in politics or in ballet. George's father, Meliton Balanchivadze, was a successful musician—a composer who specialized in folk song from his native Georgia: "The Georgian Glinka." He was a widower in his mid-forties with two grown children when he married Maria Nikolayevna Vassilyeva, a girl less than half his age. (Their son George would also marry much younger women.) Their marriage produced three children: George came between his sister, Tamara, and his brother, Andrei. It seems to have been a happy early childhood, despite financial vicissitudes—Meliton was a good-natured, generous, perhaps somewhat profligate man, who dealt with money casually when he had it and wasn't particularly perturbed when he didn't: another quality he shared with his son.

In later years Balanchine reported that after winning a huge amount of money in a state lottery, Meliton not only lost it all through extravagant generosity and foolish investments, but was prosecuted for "willful bankruptcy" and sent to debtors' prison. The children weren't told the truth, and were surprised and delighted when their father suddenly reappeared after an absence of two years. (This is the first of several bits of the Balanchine legend that may be too good to be true—the kind of romantic exaggeration he enjoyed. The more likely story, as related years later by Andrei, is that Meliton was put under house arrest as a debtor for four months.) Fortunately, although the family had to

give up their apartment in the city, they were allowed to keep their small dacha, three hours away by slow train in what is now southwestern Finland. There George spent his fifth through ninth years, studying with a tutor and taking piano lessons from a severe German lady. There was also a German nurse, who left when he was very small but whom in his old age he still recalled "with tenderness."

Meanwhile, he and his sister and brother were leading a healthy, active outdoor life in the woods surrounding the Balanchivadze home. George remembered those years with nostalgia and affection—not only this idyllic life in the country but also his earlier time in St. Petersburg. He spoke to Solomon Volkov, author of *Balanchine's Tchaikovsky,* about playing on Poklonnaya Hill, with its three ponds; about walking along the embankment of the Neva; about trips to the zoo; about how he, Tamara, and Andrei "waited impatiently for the cannon at the Fortress of Peter and Paul to boom at noon." And there was the glory of the Orthodox liturgy, which "made a wonderful impression on me when I was a child, too. The priests came out—all dressed opulently, in gorgeous miters, looking just like saints. The boys in the church choir sing so delicately, like angels." As he said to Volkov, "Childhood impressions are always the most powerful," and the beauty and power of the Orthodox liturgy never lost their hold on him.

For a family like his, the question of a secure future for the children was preeminent. Since there was very little money, a state education was essential, and the most obvious route to one for

young George was the army or navy: One of his older half-brothers was an officer, and there were other family connections to the military. When he was nine, his mother took him and his sister into St. Petersburg so that he could apply for entrance to the Imperial Naval Academy and Tamara could take the examination for the Imperial School of Ballet and Theater—she had ambitions as a dancer. At the Naval Academy they discovered that it was too late for him to apply for the current year; at the ballet school Tamara failed the exam (she had also failed it the year before, though she would pass a year later), but a casual suggestion by a passing official resulted in George's taking the exam, too—about fifty boys were trying out.

The candidates were not expected to dance. After a medical examination they had to walk back and forth before a panel of leading dancers, teachers, and administrators, who judged them by their physical appearance, their energy, their carriage. George was one of the nine boys accepted, apparently having caught the attention of an important ballerina, Olga Preobrajenska. (Again, there's another version of these events, which suggests that the year before George took the exam, his father had prepared the way by approaching the school about him. This account has less dramatic impact, but it has the ring of likelihood: As a well-known musician, Meliton would certainly have had connections at the Maryinsky. Of course, it's possible that George wasn't aware of his father's action.)

There was nothing remarkable in a child from a respectable family but without financial prospects being launched into a spe-

cialized education this way: Alexandra Danilova, for instance, who was to become George's unofficial wife during the Diaghilev years, was another such case. Not only would children like these be educated at state expense, but when they graduated after eight or nine years, they would be more or less guaranteed jobs in the ballet company itself, and eventually pensions. The Balanchivadzes' decision to take advantage of this opportunity was sensible and practical. What was remarkable was that on the very afternoon of the examination and George's acceptance in the school, his mother left him there and returned home. In the morning, he had set out to apply for the Naval Academy; in the evening, he was alone in an alien circumstance, committed to studying an art he had no interest in—he had never even *seen* a ballet. The military life, even the life of the church, had more appeal for him. Not surprisingly, he hated what had happened and immediately ran away, finding his way through the city to the home of his "Aunt" Nadia (she was actually a cousin). Knowing that this escapade could lead to instant dismissal, Nadia brought him straight back to the school and left him there.

George's first year at the theater school was an unhappy one—later he often referred to himself as having been "stuck" there ("My parents stuck me in a ballet school when I was small"). The work was basic and mechanical: During the first year, students were not exposed to actual performances and had very little notion of what they were working toward and what the drudgery of repeated exercises might lead to. He was not suc-

cessful in most of his academic subjects, receiving poor grades in everything but music and religion. And he had trouble making friends. In the early photographs of him, one can hardly miss a look of superiority, almost of disdain, certainly of wariness. The other boys called him "Rat," presumably because of the sniff—or tic—that exposed his front teeth (and that was to be a notorious physical attribute all his life). "Rat" is hardly an affectionate nickname. At one point during his early years another boy teased him so relentlessly that, as he told Bernard Taper, his first and best biographer, he "threw himself on his adversary so violently that he broke the other boy's collarbone"—a unique loss of control. Throughout his life he was known for rarely expressing his anger.

He was extremely lonely. On weekends and holidays almost all the other children went home, but his home was hours away, and apart from occasional day-trips to the dacha with Aunt Nadia, he was left in the school. Toward the end of his life he would tell Volkov, "On Saturday the school was deserted, for two days. It was sad and lonely to be left. You'd go to church and stand there for some time. . . . You had to fill time before dinner. I would go to the reception hall and play the piano. There was no one there, total emptiness." And he read a lot—the usual boys' books of the time: Jules Verne, Sherlock Holmes, Nick Carter, *The Last of the Mohicans*. All the youngest students were aware that this first year was probationary; it must have been a time for George not only of isolation and unhappiness but of tension.

Within a few years, though, he was being noticed. Danilova, a year ahead of George in the school, was to write, "I became

aware of one boy in particular—George Balanchine. He was not yet handsome, but he was interesting looking, with piercing eyes; he seemed somehow special. . . . George had a nice disposition, but while the rest of us were busy getting into mischief, he mostly kept to himself. He seemed very serious for his years." Others were aware of him, too. A young soloist in the company, Felia Doubrovska—in 1929 she would be the original Siren in Balanchine's *The Prodigal Son*—remembered noticing how intensely observant and judgmental he was, and thinking, There's a little boy who doesn't miss a thing.

In his second year, a passion for ballet was finally ignited in him: For the first time, as was usual for children at this point in their training, he was taken to the theater to participate in a performance. The ballet was *The Sleeping Beauty*. "I was Cupid, a tiny Cupid. It was Petipa's choreography. I was set down on a golden eagle. And suddenly everything opened! A crowd of people, an elegant audience. And the Maryinsky Theater all light blue and gold! And suddenly the orchestra started playing. I sat on the cage in indescribable ecstasy enjoying it all—the music, the theater, and the fact that I was onstage. Thanks to *Sleeping Beauty* I fell in love with ballet."

He was not the only one for whom this was true. *Sleeping Beauty* was the work that crystallized in both Anna Pavlova and the artist Léon Bakst their passion for ballet. Stravinsky loved Tchaikovsky's great score. Diaghilev more or less bankrupted his company by mounting *Sleeping Beauty* in London for three months in 1921. And one could argue that what fully awakened

the United States to the grandeur of classical ballet was the triumph of Margot Fonteyn as *Beauty*'s Aurora during the first New York season, in 1949, of the Sadler's Wells Ballet. Balanchine's love for *The Sleeping Beauty* would last his entire life: In his final years he was still contemplating presenting it at the New York City Ballet.

From then on George appeared in countless ballets at the Maryinsky. He was in the dance sequences of Tchaikovsky's operas *The Queen of Spades* and *Eugene Onegin*, and he took part in Petipa's *The Pharaoh's Daughter*; that was the first time he received an anonymous credit, "Monkey—A Student," a role in which he scampered about in the trees and for which, he told Taper, he had a special affinity. He was in other Petipa ballets, of course—*Raymonda* (an Arab boy), *Don Quixote* (a Spanish boy), *Paquita, Esmeralda, The Corsair*. He was in *Swan Lake* and *The Nutcracker*. "Yes, I was in it," he said about the latter, when in 1954 he created his version for City Ballet: "Mouse, Hoop—everything, just like everybody else." In fact, his most successful role as a student was in the Hoop Dance, which he would re-create in his own production as "Candy Canes," in a sequence, he went out of his way to say, that was "absolutely authentic, from Russia." That this role was a specialty of his confirms Danilova's recollection that "his distinguishing features . . . were speed, musicality, a big jump, and a sharp attack," and that he was destined to end up as a character dancer rather than as a *danseur noble*. He did, though, also

appear in *Nutcracker* as the Child-Prince, whose mime he was to reproduce, unchanged, decades later.

During his years in the school, Balanchine was working hard at becoming a musician, practicing whenever he could find the time (and a piano). This eventually led to his being invited by senior students to accompany them during school graduation performances, which in turn led to his being noticed by teachers, dancers, and the school administrators. In 1919 he entered the Conservatory of Music, which was under the direction of Alexander Glazunov, the renowned composer of *Raymonda*. There he studied not only piano but harmony, counterpoint, and composition. He also experimented with the violin, the French horn, the drums, and the trumpet. His professor of piano, Sofia Frantsevna Zurmullen, appraised him thus:

> Talented and very musical. He worked under the most difficult conditions. For the first year and a half he was a pupil of the State Ballet School, did not have his own instrument, and could only play in the large theater hall, which involved great inconveniences. Finishing the school, he continued to live there under the same conditions and only in March of this year [1922] did he acquire an instrument for himself. His ballet activity left him exhausted. . . . I hope that he will be able to finish the Conservatory successfully.

This he never did, but as the dance historian Yuri Slonimsky—a close friend from this period—summed it up: "Balanchine in those years made himself into a professional musician."

He was also beginning to choreograph. When he was sixteen, in 1920, he received permission to create a *pas de deux* for the annual school performance—*La Nuit*, set to a romance by Anton Rubinstein. According to Danilova, it was "a sexy number," involving a revolutionary one-arm lift in arabesque. The girl was Olga Mungalova, with whom he fell in love— "She had exquisitely beautiful legs. Every acrobatic trick was a snap for her." Mikhail Baryshnikov has reported that *La Nuit* was still being performed in Russia in his day. In 1921, when George was graduated (with honors) from the school, he followed the standard path into the Maryinsky *corps de ballet*, with a clear future in the company ahead of him—if he chose to accept it. But events, both in the dance world and the larger world, were to make that path unacceptable to him.

Balanchine's later years in ballet school coincided with the outbreak of World War I and the Russian Revolution. Toward the end of 1917, the year of the Revolution, both the school and the company were shut down. The country was experiencing civil war, and the quick succession of governments—from czarist to Kerensky's socialism to Lenin's communism—resulted in chaos and severe deprivation. George's father had left for Tiflis (now Tbilisi), where he was to become minister of culture in what was momentarily the Republic of Georgia. With the school shut, George moved in with his mother, sister, and brother, but in early 1918, his family left St. Petersburg (renamed Petrograd) to join his father. George, just fourteen, was never to see his parents or his sister again.

While waiting for the school to reopen, he was living a hand-to-mouth existence with Aunt Nadia, scrounging for food like everyone else. Slonimsky sums up the period: "The civil war, the blockade . . . Petrograd, it seemed, was dying. The streets were empty, the windows of inactive shops were boarded up or broken. Transport . . . often came to a halt for lack of electricity and gasoline. Lights often went out, throwing the streets and apartments into darkness. Hunger and cold tormented everyone." George took any job he could find—playing piano for silent films, messenger boy, saddler's assistant—working not for money but "for whatever scraps of food his employers could spare or for . . . some matches or some soap, perhaps, that might be bartered for a crust of bread." He would walk for miles to find peasants in the countryside with whom he could trade salt he had saved for potatoes. With some other students he would steal from government supplies—if apprehended, they could have been executed—and cats were regularly caught, strangled, and cooked. "Sometimes we were given horse feed," Danilova remembers. "The horses, meanwhile, were dropping dead in the streets. During the night, people would come with knives and take whatever they could from the carcasses; in the morning there would be only bones." Naturally everyone was hungry, she writes, "and began to develop boils—at one time I had five, but that was nothing compared with George, who had thirty."

In 1918 Anatoly Lunacharsky, the Bolshevik commissar of education, succeeded in convincing Lenin that ballet was not a decadent art but something from which the proletariat might

benefit. The school and the theater were reopened, but performances were at first limited to interludes at long, intense political meetings—Taper reports that Balanchine, forty years later, could still "give a telling imitation, both ludicrous and frightening, of a Trotsky harangue he once heard from the Maryinsky wings." When regular performances finally resumed, the audience sat in the freezing theater—there was no fuel to heat it. "The water froze in the pipes and they burst," Balanchine told Volkov. "Ice floated in the sinks. The corps de ballet wore long-sleeved T-shirts under their costumes. But what could the poor prima dancers do? They got pneumonia, one after the other."

What in all likelihood kept Balanchine, whose health was delicate, from physical breakdown during this long period of deprivation was his introduction to the family of a young girl he first met in 1920. Her name was Tamara Zheverzheyeva, later Gevergeyeva, ultimately Geva. When he fell in love with her, about two years later, she was fifteen and he was three years older. Tamara—a beautiful, lively ash blonde—wasn't a product of the state school but was taking classes there at night. They began to see each other and perform together in nightclubs around the city—at times Tamara would sing to George's accompaniment. Then, as Geva put it, "As time rolled on, our friendship gave way to a more intimate relationship." By then Balanchine had moved into the large Zheverzheyev apartment. The father had made a fortune from manufacturing religious objects and cloth, owned a vast collection of valuable books, and had built an experimental theater and a museum, which he was

being allowed by the Bolsheviks to run, although most of his property had been confiscated: Under the new regime there was no need for religious artifacts.

Tamara's father took to George, who had (she would one day write) "so many qualities that Father admired—talent, nonconformity, the determination to follow his own course and convictions despite any opposition." He also enjoyed George's piano playing, particularly of Wagner. And he was happy to give George a place to stay and food to eat. According to Tamara, one day her father said to the two young people, "Why don't you get married? I mean it. It is obvious that you are crazy about each other. Whether it is puppy love or a real one doesn't matter. Time will settle that. If you find out it was a mistake, you can always get a divorce. Meanwhile, I would feel easier if you were married." "Why not!" George said. "Why not!" Tamara echoed. That's how it came about, she wrote, "and I challenge anyone to match this romantic proposal." Actually, George himself was to challenge it decades later, telling Volkov, "I heard a story going around that it was Zheverzheyev's idea that Tamara and I get married. Nothing of the kind, it never happened. Zheverzheyev paid no attention to Tamara and me, he was totally engrossed in his unique collection. I lived at the Zheverzheyev house; I had nowhere else to go. . . . Zheverzheyev demanded Wagner of me, that's true. But to marry Tamara, no. Tamara and I got married on our own." Who knows? Geva's memoirs, *Split Seconds*, are charmingly written but somewhat fanciful. Yet presumably the scrupulous Bernard Taper, who repeats her story, heard it from

Balanchine as well as from her. What's certain is that at the end of his life, Balanchine didn't *want* it to be true.

Although Balanchine's domestic life was now more set-tled—eventually he and his wife moved out of her family home and into a small apartment of their own—his artistic life had reached a critical juncture: Would he attach himself to the conservative forces at the Maryinsky, or would he strike out in his own direction? Ferment in the world of choreography had begun long before the Revolution, with the work of Alexander Gorsky at the Bolshoi Theater in Moscow and of Fokine in St. Petersburg. Balanchine admired Fokine's *Chopiniana* (*Les Sylphides* to us, although when New York City Ballet staged it in 1972, it was presented under its original name). He would have seen *The Dying Swan, Le Carnaval,* and other early Fokine works, and he himself danced in *La Jota Aragonese* and as one of the Polovtsians in *Prince Igor.* But the chief influences on him during his early years as a choreographer were Fedor Lopukhov and Kasian Goleizovsky, Lopukhov because of the way he approached dance through music, Goleizovsky because of his radical experiments in advancing dance vocabulary. In 1923 Lopukhov staged a big pure-dance ballet called *The Magnificence of the Universe,* to Beethoven's Fourth Symphony, in whose only performance (it was a fiasco) Balanchine appeared, together with several of his closest colleagues. The Soviet dance historian Elizabeth Souritz quotes Lopukhov writing about what he calls "dancing the music" as opposed to dancing "close to the music," "to the music," and "in the music." "Naturally," Souritz writes, "such an approach assumes analyzing the musical score, break-

ing it down into its constituent elements, and then searching for the equivalent movements for each element." And she points out how important it would be to Balanchine to follow Petipa and Lopukhov in seeing dance composition "as an analogue to musical composition, beyond literary conjectures, dramatic concretization, and subjective interpretations."*

Kasian Goleizovsky was important not only because he created unprecedented radical movements and poses, but because they were founded on strict classical precepts. In other words, like Balanchine but well before him, he was expanding the language of classical ballet while adhering to it. "Bold variations on traditional positions were created," Souritz writes. "The ballerina executed arabesques and attitudes not standing up, but up in the air, in the arms of her partner, and sometimes sitting or lying down."

A contemporary critic wrote of Goleizovsky's startling vocabulary, "An unexpected function has been given to the leg—to serve not as support for the body, but as an independently expressive factor. . . . The leg 'gesticulates.' Through the interweaving of the lines of the arms and legs, new and unusual effects are obtained." This, too, anticipates Balanchine, who on attending a performance of Goleizovsky's Chamber Ballet group, "rushed backstage to express his enthusiasm to the choreographer." "Seeing Goleizovsky," he told Taper, "was what first gave me the courage to try something different on my own."

. . .

The Magnificence of the Universe was crudely reconstructed at the Maryinsky in 2004 and proved to be a rather awkward and obvious piece of avant-gardism. Yet one could see that Balanchine might have been influenced by it.

By 1923 Balanchine was choreographing all kinds of things in all kinds of places. Slonimsky remembers that "his friends and fellow dancers were pestering him, 'George! Tell me what to dance! Help adapt this old piece!! Arrange a dance for me to this music!' And Balanchine, who always found it extremely difficult to say no, would try to satisfy these requests on the spot." Around him sprung up a group of young dancers who came to be known as the Young Ballet. They included his old girlfriend Mungalova, Danilova, Lidia Ivanova, Pyotr Gusev, Nikolai "Kola" Efimov, and eventually his wife. Artists and musicians were associated with the group as well. They gave concerts wherever they could find a venue, Balanchine composing dances for a production of Rimsky-Korsakov's *Le Coq d'or,* for plays by Schnitzler, Toller, even Shaw's *Caesar and Cleopatra.* Quickly, the Young Ballet became famous—or notorious. Old-guard critics were dismissive; avant-garde or merely open-minded judges were enthusiastic. Balanchine became a central figure in the radical art movements of the day, his picture on the cover of the influential magazine *Theater.* At that time he was in a Chopin phase—wearing black, his hair plastered down over his forehead, his expression mournful, although in private he remained fun-loving and, indeed, funny. For the Young Ballet he choreographed a solemn piece to Chopin's *Marche Funèbre*—according to Geva, "twelve youngsters in stark linen tunics, our heads encased in tight hoods, building a design of uncompromising grief to the dark downbeat, changing from the mourners into the dead, into whirling spirits, our bodies twisting into arches and crosses." For the same program he made another dance set to a rhythmic recitation of Russian limericks.

These were not performances that brought in much money, yet Slonimsky remembers that whatever George earned from the Young Ballet, he would share with those in the group who were needier. He had his salary from the ballet company, but it was small, and not much came in from his and Tamara's night-club acts. More important to him was that despite his growing reputation, the authorities at the theater were not only reluctant to give him choreographic assignments (they refused his request to stage Stravinsky's *Sacre du printemps*) but were actively discouraging other members of the company from dancing for him. According to Danilova, "We were summoned by the Maryinsky directors. If we continued to work with Balanchine, we would be expelled, they threatened. Balanchine they didn't even warn—he was expelled from the theatre, then and there, as punishment for his experiments." He may not have minded this much: He was certainly more interested in making dances than in dancing—Geva claims that he actually *hated* dancing, though that was not the general view. And however willing he may have been to take on assignments, he was utterly independent when it came to how he would fulfill them.

His strong religious impulses, his resentment of authority, his fragile health undermined by the privations of the past half-dozen years, and undoubtedly a young man's instinct for adventure and change—all combined to ignite his desire to get out of Bolshevik Russia. He was also, by then, almost fully cut off from his family in Georgia. "It was impossible living in Russia," he told Volkov. "It was horrible—nothing to eat, people in the West can't even understand what that means. We were hungry all the

time. We dreamed of going away, anywhere, as long as we got away. To go or not to go—I never had any doubts at all. None! I never doubted, I always knew: if I ever had the chance, I'd go."

He was not the only one thinking this way. Vladimir Dimitriev, a onetime singer of light opera, was now raking it in (for himself) as a croupier in a private gambling club. "A very clever, calculating man," Geva called him. He proposed that they form a small group for a summer tour abroad, and Danilova, George and Tamara, and Danilova's frequent partner Kola Efimov were enlisted, along with the talented Lidia Ivanova. Dimitriev, through his high government contacts, was able to convince the authorities that his ambition was to help educate some talented young people by taking them on a two-month tour of Germany—at his own expense, of course. It would also be an opportunity to give Europe a glimpse of Soviet culture. "For days," Geva wrote, "we behaved as if we'd been hit by lightning."

And then, shortly before the planned departure, Lidia Ivanova died in a highly suspicious boating accident. She had been close—too close, the others felt—to certain officers in the GPU (the secret police) and knew too much. This tragedy only made the others more anxious to get away, although Danilova, at least, believed she would be back at the Maryinsky after the summer—she had, after all, been promised the leading role of Kitri in Petipa's *Don Quixote*.

Sometime in late June 1924, the four dancers, shepherded by Dimitriev, boarded a steamship in Leningrad (the latest name for St. Petersburg) bound for the East Prussian port of Stettin.

Until the ship was well out of range of the Soviet authorities, they did not relax—there had been the usual last-minute red tape about their papers. "George alone is calm," Geva wrote. "He is deeply religious and has the unshakable conviction that God is always at his side to help him, whatever his need may be."

However badly he had wanted to leave Russia, though, and however strong his faith in God, Balanchine might have been shaken had he known that it would be thirty-eight years before he would see his homeland again: shaken, but not surprised. Above all, he believed in fate. Slonimsky recalled an acrostic on his name, "Balanchivadze," which George wrote as a child, the last syllables of the Russian words corresponding to the separate elements of his name:

> *Fate smiles on me.*
> *I am Ba.*
> *My destiny in life is fixed*
> *I am Lan.*
> *I see the keys to success.*
> *I am Chi.*
> *I will not turn back now,*
> *I am Vad.*
> *In spite of storm or tempest.*
> *I am Ze.*

IN THE TWENTIES

Above: In Venice, 1926   *Right:* Portrait by Vladimir Dimitriev

Chapter Two

With Diaghilev

Even the boat trip from Leningrad to Stettin was a revelation to the four dancers and Dimitriev. To begin with, there was food. "The supply of bread seemed unlimited," Danilova wrote. "We would wrap up a few extra rolls in our napkins and smuggle them back to our rooms, just in case we got hungry. We had forgotten what it felt like to be full." And then everything was so clean, so neat—so German. From Stettin they moved on to Berlin—the Berlin of the Weimar Republic. To the members of the "Soviet State Dancers," Berlin seemed alive, luxurious, decadent. It was not, however, interested in four unknown Russian dancers with amateurish costumes, sets, and piano accompaniment. After a month of waiting, there was one disastrous performance in a gloomy hall. Danilova and Efimov did classical excerpts, Tamara and George some "modern" dances. The management canceled the second scheduled performance. And money was running out. Geva had her beautiful ash-blonde hair cut off and sold it to a wigmaker.

Eventually, through a local impresario the group began a series of recitals in towns along the Rhine. According to Geva,

"We danced in dingy halls, in summer theatres, on open stages, in ballrooms for private parties, in beer gardens and for the inmates of an insane asylum. . . . Our last appearance was in a vaudeville show in a Mainz beer garden. Birds flew overhead, the stage was slippery, and the hale and hearty audience was drinking beer and occasionally bursting into song. We followed a dog act."

By this time summer was almost over and they were due to return to Russia, but going back to the privations and restrictions of life in Leningrad was unthinkable. When a telegram arrived from home demanding their immediate return, only Danilova hesitated—after all, she had *Don Quixote* to go back to. But when a booking at London's Empire Theatre materialized for November, she decided that she wasn't ready for the adventure in the West to be over. The contracts from London arrived, and "in the end, I signed." George, of course, had no doubts; as Geva put it, "We had had a taste of the world and we wanted more. Come what may, we were going to stay."

London proved to be as big a fiasco as Berlin. The Empire was a vaudeville house, not the Maryinsky Theater; none of the dancers spoke English; and they didn't understand the pace and precision required by vaudeville performances. After two weeks they were fired. Since they had no work, they couldn't stay in England. Only France offered refuge for the stateless, so (as Geva put it) "Paris it was."

There are various versions of what happened there. The most dramatic, naturally, is Geva's: They take rooms in a cheap hotel on the Place de la République; they are completely unknown;

they have no money; Dimitriev has a brainstorm: "Why don't we risk our money on a trip to Monte Carlo, to see Diaghilev? The company is there, getting ready for the season. Maybe he'll give you kids a job." But there isn't enough money to get them back to Paris if Diaghilev fails them. Only George is philosophical; when Tamara asks him what they should do, he answers, "Nothing. We wait."

Suddenly there's a knock on the door and the concierge announces, *"Téléphone pour Monsieur George."*

"A look of astonishment passed between us. We didn't know a soul in Paris and had certainly not been seen anywhere. Puzzled, we waited for George to come back. When he walked in, he was pale and spoke slowly. 'It was Diaghilev,' he said. 'His agents traced us from London, and it took them five days to find us in Paris.' He took a deep breath. 'He wants to see us all tomorrow.'" They were to audition for him at the home of his great friend and supporter Misia Sert.

According to Danilova, however, Diaghilev had succeeded in tracking them down in London, where his advance man delivered a note, inviting them to Paris. "Well, of course we were very flattered." Taper, more or less confirming Danilova, states that Diaghilev sent them a telegram and transportation money, requesting them to come to Paris for an audition. In his biography of Balanchine, Richard Buckle, more or less confirming Geva, repeats the cheap-hotel-telephone-call account. Since everyone in the ballet world always knows everything that's happening everywhere, it is highly plausible that Diaghilev's connections in

Leningrad would have alerted him to the presence in Europe of four promising young dancers from the Maryinsky—his Ballets Russes was always greedy for talented classical dancers. It's also plausible, as some have suggested, that his young associate Boris Kochno and Anton Dolin, then an important Diaghilev dancer, had spotted the little troupe in London and recognized their potential.

Whatever the circumstances, the fateful encounter between Balanchine and Diaghilev finally took place. Danilova was slightly piqued when asked to demonstrate her dancing—wasn't she a soloist at the Maryinsky? Balanchine, on the other hand, was happy to demonstrate his ability to create dances. Diaghilev was badly in need of a choreographer, particularly for the opera ballets he was obliged to turn out for the Monte Carlo opera company, and Balanchine assured him that he could make opera ballets "very fast." The four dancers were hired. A few days later, in London, Balanchine taught his *Marche Funèbre* to some of the Ballets Russes dancers to show Diaghilev what he could do, and soon after that—when Diaghilev's resident choreographer, Bronislava Nijinska, left the company—Balanchine was given her job. As Taper eloquently summed up, "Thus it happened that at the age of twenty Georgi Melotonovitch Balanchivadze—or George Balanchine, as he would henceforth be known—found himself ballet master of the most famous and remarkable ballet company in the world."

The great impresario Serge Diaghilev had galvanized the artistic and social worlds of Paris in 1909 with his Saison Russe at the

Théâtre du Châtelet. (The year before, he had revealed Chaliapin to Paris in *Boris Godunov.*) Stravinsky's dissonant music, Léon Bakst and Alexandre Benois' dazzling lavish sets, the thrilling Nijinsky, the enchanting Karsavina, the ineffable Pavlova (until she set off on her eternal mission to bring dance to the world, no company or impresario big enough to contain her), the ballets of Fokine—*Les Sylphides, The Firebird, Petrouchka, Schéhérazade, The Polovtsian Dances* from *Prince Igor*—made the early Ballets Russes seasons wildly successful, first in Paris, then in London. By 1924, however, Fokine was long gone, as was his successor, Léonide Massine, although he would make return appearances when needed. Nijinsky was gone, too, after contributing *L'Après-midi d'un faune, Jeux,* and the scandalous *Le Sacre du printemps,* then betraying Diaghilev by marrying. And Nijinska, despite her successes with *Les Noces* and *Les Biches,* was now gone as well.

Although the early triumphs were still in the repertory, and popular, Diaghilev had tired of Russian primitivism and orientalist dance-drama and had turned to a French aesthetic: Ravel, Satie, Poulenc, Milhaud, Auric, Cocteau, Chanel, as well as the School of Paris artists—Matisse, Derain, Laurençin, the adopted Frenchman Picasso—whom he was now employing to create his decor in place of Bakst and Benois. Stravinsky, too, was growing more Westernized. Ballets Russes audiences, particularly in Paris, had been conditioned always to expect something new, and it would now be up to Balanchine to provide it.

His first task, however, was to deal with the opera ballets that needed enlivening. Responsibility for these was an important

element of Diaghilev's arrangement with the principality of Monaco, and they had to be taken seriously. Most opera ballet is standardized doodling; although he had almost no experience with opera ballets, Balanchine threw himself into the job with his usual energy, efficiency, and ability. The dancers were delighted, as dancers always are with choreographers who extend their possibilities and make them look good. And Balanchine made them *feel* good as well; he radiated confidence without self-importance, and he was fun to be around. "How refreshing was his originality!" wrote Ninette de Valois, then in Diaghilev's *corps de ballet*. "His great musical sense never failed to make the most of the material offered to him, even when confronted with that outlet so universally dreaded by all choreographers—the opera-ballet." And she recalls "the first time he ever arranged anything. It was a pas de trois in some opera for myself, Doubrovska and Danilova. And I remember coming into the dressing room after, and saying, 'I think he's a genius.'"

In his first half year alone, he prepared dances for sixteen productions, from *La Traviata* to *Carmen* to *Manon* to *The Fair at Sorotchinsk*. In just two months early in 1926, Buckle tells us, he turned out "a polonaise for *Boris Godunov,* dances for Honegger's *Judith,* a Hindu number for *Lakmé,* a waltz and pas de deux for *Les Contes d'Hoffman,* and 'medieval' dances for Gounod's *Jeanne d'Arc.*" His most important work in opera was for the world premiere of the Ravel-Colette *L'Enfant et les sortilèges*—a piece he would return to repeatedly in the course of his career. His work was so new and alive that Monaco audiences were beginning to

go to the opera to look at the dancing—an infrequent phenomenon in twentieth-century opera history. He was learning from
all this handiwork, too: "From Verdi's way of dealing with the
chorus," he was to say, "I learned how to handle the *corps de
ballet*, the ensemble, the soloists—how to make the soloists stand
out against the *corps de ballet* and when to give them time to
rest." His work in Russia had consisted almost entirely of duets
or small ensemble pieces; an actual *corps de ballet* was a new challenge, and one he met easily and quickly.

Diaghilev, impressed, gave him his first major commission—
to rework from scratch a ballet to Stravinsky's *Le Chant du
rossignol*, with which Massine had failed some years before but
whose original Matisse costumes the company still held in stor-
age. This venture was auspicious in several ways. On the advice
of Anton Dolin, Diaghilev and Balanchine had gone to the
London studio of Serafina Astafieva to observe a fourteen-year-
old girl with amazing technical ability. She was Lillian Alicia
Marks, who was hired immediately to be Stravinsky's Nightin-
gale and quickly renamed Alicia Markova. Balanchine also used
her in *L'Enfant et les sortilèges*. ("He had me pirouetting like mad
out of the fireplace; and in the second scene I was the little squir-
rel. I used to turn like a top, which George adored.")

More significant was that *Rossignol* led to Balanchine's first
encounters with Stravinsky, beginning a relationship that was to
have as much consequence for the history of ballet as did Petipa's
with Tchaikovsky. "Stravinsky played the music on the piano,"
Balanchine recalled. "The tempi was absolutely right . . . Diaghilev

comes—with cane, with monocle—he sits, he listens. He wants everything faster, faster, faster. I change everything for him. Then Stravinsky comes and says, 'Didn't I tell you slower, slower?'" Balanchine listened to Stravinsky, as he would go on doing for the rest of the composer's life—through *Apollo, Orpheus, Agon,* and the other masterpieces they created together.

During this time Balanchine was also dancing a wide variety of roles. Opinions differ as to how good he was. Tamara Geva acknowledges that he was a good dancer, "light and wiry." Boris Kochno, Diaghilev's secretary and the librettist for such ballets as *The Prodigal Son* and *Cotillon*—a man with a good eye—says, "In the few ballets he danced, Balanchine was wonderful," though he adds, "He liked to be comical, and sometimes he overdid it." De Valois says he was "terrible." To Markova, whom he frequently partnered in *Aurora's Wedding,* he "was a wonderful dancer. He had such elegance and he was a marvelous partner, showing off his ballerina so beautifully." After 1927, when he sustained an injury to his knee and underwent an unsuccessful operation, he mostly limited himself to character roles—old men in *The Three-Cornered Hat* and *Petrouchka,* the King of Spades in *La Boutique fantasque*. In his own *Triumph of Neptune* he performed a solo as a black servant named Snowball. The historian Cyril Beaumont described it as "a dance full of subtly contrasted rhythms, strutting walks, mincing steps, and surging backward bendings of the body, borrowed from the cakewalk, the whole invested with a delicious humor." Geva tells us that he adored makeup: "The less he looked like himself, the more he loved it." He was admired by

everybody for his thrilling performance of the *lezghinka,* a Georgian folk dance, and by all accounts he was highly effective as Kastchei, the evil magician in Fokine's *Firebird.* As late as 1930, bad knee and all, he performed (in Copenhagen) Nijinsky's old role in *Le Spectre de la rose,* slightly modified, and according to his partner, Ulla Poulsen, "did it very well." His own view of his dancing? "I was, as a matter of fact," he told Taper, "a wonderful dancer."

Life in the Diaghilev company took on a pleasant rhythm—annual seasons in Monte Carlo, Paris, London, with occasional short seasons in various European countries. Most of the creative work was accomplished in Monte Carlo. Among Balanchine's young friends, often on hand, were Vladimir Dukelsky (Vernon Duke), who was composing a score for Diaghilev (and had a big crush on Geva), and the great violinist Nathan Milstein and *his* close friend from Russia, Vladimir Horowitz. There were the usual comings and goings, rivalries and scandals, crises, triumphs, and disasters—all the parodies of life in a Russian ballet company are essentially true to life. But the serious work never faltered: Diaghilev knew just what he wanted and ruthlessly exacted it from his colleagues. He observed everything, oversaw everything, interfered with everything. When a dancer gave a less than first-rate performance, he or she was informed of it coldly by Diaghilev himself, or through his trusted *régisseur,* Serge Grigoriev. Conductors were given strict orders about tempi. Diaghilev himself often took a hand in the lighting.

Composers—he was an experienced musician—were advised on what was wrong with their commissioned scores, and ordered to make fixes. (He demanded so many changes in the score for *Le Bal* that Vittorio Rieti, the composer, finally wrote to him, "Dear Monsieur Diaghilev, Here is *Le Bal*. It is dedicated to you; it belongs to you; do anything you want to with it, but above all, don't dream of my working for you again! Yours, always . . .")

The extent to which Diaghilev supervised Balanchine's work is hard to judge. Certainly he controlled all aspects of decor, costume, lighting, music. But from the first he accorded Balanchine a large measure of independence about the actual choreography. Diaghilev knew that he himself was not a choreographer, but with Nijinsky, Massine, and Nijinska he had been dealing with beginners whom he himself had more or less invented. When Balanchine joined the Ballets Russes, however, he was already a choreographer with his own ideas and methods—someone whom Diaghilev could employ, educate, and advise, but whom he couldn't invent or even inspire. Nor did they ever become personally close—possibly because Balanchine had no ambition to be part of the inner circle, possibly because he was hopelessly heterosexual.

In his discreet but convincing memoirs, *The Diaghilev Ballet 1909–1929*, Grigoriev tells a curious story. At the end of the 1928 season, after Balanchine's success with *La Chatte* and *Apollon Musagète*, among others, Diaghilev

> astounded me by fiercely abusing Balanchine: he felt very much, he said, like not renewing his contract at all! What the cause of this sudden change was I could not fathom. But

I forbore to ask questions and merely said that all I wished to know was whether he proposed to retain Balanchine or not. If he did, then I would arrange the contract myself. "Do as you like," said Diaghilev, after a pause—and so, to my relief, since, with Massine gone, Balanchine was our sole stand-by for choreography, the contract was safely renewed.

Grigoriev does not go on to speculate about the reasons for this outburst, but it hardly seems a rational one, since every successful ballet in the repertory after 1925 was Balanchine's. Or perhaps that was the very reason. Autocrats are not always grateful to underlings who appear to be indispensable. Diaghilev had been equally ruthless about the loss of Fokine, whose work was the foundation of the Ballets Russes, and then of his main attraction, Nijinsky, when he asserted his independence by marrying.

Balanchine's humor and good nature were remarked on by almost everybody—obviously a welcome change after his complicated and demanding predecessors. "He has a most extraordinary sense of humor," reported the leading dancer Lydia Sokolova (née Hilda Munnings). "He can tell stories for hours and hours and hours and not be tired. And the same with his work; it bubbles." De Valois wrote, "We loved him because he was such a relaxed person. Quite beyond his being so brilliant, he was so easy, you were never nervous when you were working with him. . . . He was a friend, you were working for a friend." And de Valois told Moira Shearer (of *Red Shoes* fame) that in company class, "He was always at the back, giggling and messing

around." Vernon Duke, in his racy autobiography, refers to him as "the Tiflis pixie," and recalls that "George, probably the most lovable creature who ever lived, was already his well-known unpredictable self—mixing sheer lunacy with phlegmatic laissez-aller, carried to unheard-of lengths." Balanchine, he also tells us, liked playing the guitar and, in his primitive English, singing his own version of a current pop success: "Everybohdy lohves my bohdy, but my bohdy lohves nobohdy but me." Well, he *was* only twenty-one.

Certainly we get the impression of a happy temperament, a hard worker, a good companion. Life in Monte Carlo was a lot of fun—the wonderful weather, the good food, *l'amour*. These were the Roaring Twenties, after all, and this was the Riviera. Milstein remembers how they all palled around together—he, Horowitz, Balanchine, and Danilova: "Everyone around us fell in love, came together, broke up."

Indeed, Balanchine and Geva had broken up. She was a talented dancer, but not on the level of Danilova or the other ballerinas, and Diaghilev had made it clear that he had no big plans for her. Her George was becoming central to the company, while she was peripheral. She went to Paris on her own—George didn't seem to notice. She came back, to better roles. She took a lover—a Spanish marquis, "handsome, rich, titled, intelligent, selective," and "crazy about me." (And married.) Soon, however, her position deteriorated again—Diaghilev was featuring Alice Nikitina, whose lover, Lord Rothermere, was financing the company. And George had taken up with "Choura" Danilova. When Geva heard

that the famous theatrical revue company the Chauve-Souris was looking for new talent, she offered herself and was snapped up for their forthcoming American tour. George obligingly created three special numbers for her, which proved to be a sensation in New York. (She was always proud that it was she who introduced his work to America.) Late in his life, Balanchine told Volkov, "The first time I got married, I was young, I didn't care in the least. Married . . . so we're married. Then we both went abroad. And there, you look around, and there are so many marvelous women. And my wife [Geva] began moving away from our life, our Russian life. She spoke French and German, you know. She kept wanting to go somewhere, see something, do something. I sensed that she had developed new interests. And then I thought, time to end all this." Easy come, easy go.

That was in retrospect. Some years before his sessions with Volkov, he had acknowledged to Taper that he had been hurt by Geva's departure, "but not mortally." Danilova, "the other woman," tells an entirely different story in her memoirs, however. One evening in London, "George came to my room to massage my foot for me." Then he kissed it. She was "a little taken aback, but then I thought, well, it's just an affectionate gesture." A week or so later she asks Kola Efimov why George seems so sad. Kola says, "Ask him." When she says that she *has* asked him, Kola tells her, "Ask him again." "So I asked him once again, and he said, 'Well, don't you know? I love you.' 'No, it can't be,' I said. 'How? What about Tamara?' 'Well,' he said, 'I don't love her.'"

She's shocked, she's perturbed—and all the more so when she overhears Tamara saying, "One of my best friends is taking away my husband." When George tells Tamara how he feels, Choura can see that Tamara "was very hurt" yet unwilling to stay with him if he didn't love her any longer. George grows more and more insistent with Choura, threatening to go away—to America. ("I have an offer.") Choura thinks hard. "We had known each other since we were nine years old" (actually, she was ten when they met), "we had watched each other grow up, we had danced together. In *Tannhäuser* at the Maryinsky, in the Venusberg scene, we had been paired together for the Bacchanale; the choreography called for us to embrace. And then, I remember, for the first time, my heart quickened." After further reflection, "I decided that I loved him, that I wanted to be with him." Unfortunately, when they all left Russia together, George and Tamara hadn't brought their marriage papers with them, so they couldn't at that point get a divorce. Tamara gone, Choura moves in, "happy to be with him but crying because I had always dreamed of being a bride and walking down the aisle in a long white dress." The odd circumstance of the missing marriage papers is why Danilova is generally referred to either as the second of Balanchine's five wives, which she wasn't legally, or as his "unofficial" wife. (Since they seemed to consider themselves married during their time together, and others did too, I count her among the wives.)

Once the company got over this "scandalous" state of affairs, Choura was presented everywhere as George's wife—and no one

ever asked for documents. Their life together was smooth and pleasant. Not only was George easy to get along with—there was never a quarrel—and extremely generous, but "ours was not the kind of relationship in which we would bare our souls—there was no need to, because we had known each other since childhood. . . . In a way, we were each other's best friends." One could put it another way: Danilova was the closest thing to a family that Balanchine now had.

But undoubtedly of central importance to the relationship was the fact that Danilova was an extremely talented dancer, with wit, elegance, and very beautiful legs—they were to become as famous in the world of ballet as Dietrich's were in the world of film. With her Maryinsky classical training (she had excelled as a student) and her attractive stage presence, she was an important addition to the Diaghilev company, even if she was not immediately placed front and center. Like everyone else, she was thrown into countless opera ballets, but Balanchine used her modestly in *Barabau,* his first work after the success of *Le Chant du rossignol,* and then—in blackface—in a minor effort called *Jack in the Box.* Her breakthrough came in the pageantlike affair called *The Triumph of Neptune,* put together especially for London at the end of 1926; Diaghilev was obeying his English patron, Lord Rothermere, by mounting a ballet with a British theme. The score was commissioned from Lord Berners, the libretto was by Sacheverell Sitwell, and the sets were suggested by colorful Victorian toy theaters. (Boris Kochno remembered going with Diaghilev to an obscure London shop and spending

whole days with him, "shuffling through dusty piles of countless engravings of such pantomime sets as 'Jack and the Giant Killer,' 'The Forty Thieves,' and 'The Silver Palace.'") Danilova recalled that Balanchine employed the same revolutionary one-arm lift that had startled the audience at his very first ballet, *La Nuit*, back in school. (He was always in the recycling business.) She also did a hornpipe to great applause, and the whole venture proved to be Balanchine's greatest success to date.

Of Diaghilev's last eleven ballets, eight were choreographed by Balanchine, four of them of major importance. By this time Diaghilev had a new favorite, the very good-looking Serge Lifar, whom Nijinska had imported from Kiev and who, at first, was barely adequate. He was immensely ambitious, though, and immensely hardworking, and in a few years he had become the company's principal male dancer. He played a leading role in *Barabau*; the telegraph boy to Doubrovska's film star in *La Pastorale*; the hero (Tom Tug the Sailor) in *The Triumph of Neptune*. But it was in Balanchine's 1927 *La Chatte* that he became a star. This work, based on an Aesop fable, told the story of a cat turned into a woman and the man in love with her, who dies of disappointment when, revealing her true nature, she chases off after a mouse. The cat was the great ballerina Olga Spessivtseva, whom Diaghilev and Balanchine both adored, despite her famous lack of musicality. Lifar was the lover, and Balanchine revealed his androgynous beauty while cannily masking his technical weaknesses. *La Chatte* was a big success, although as usual in

those days most of the credit went to the aspects of the ballet that Diaghilev controlled: the libretto, the music, and especially the Constructivist sets by Naum Gabo and Antoine Pevsner, as well as the startling costumes, partly made out of celluloid. Choreographers were rarely hailed as the heroes of Diaghilev's successes.

Le Bal, with decor by Giorgio de Chirico, was another success—the first work in which Balanchine used a ball or party as a setting: *Cotillon, La Sonnambula, La Valse, Liebeslieder Waltzer, Vienna Waltzes* were to come. Danilova, who recalled the steps as being "very syncopated," had another triumph, but, as she reports in her memoirs, at the premiere, in Monte Carlo, she was the only soloist who didn't receive flowers. Diaghilev asked Balanchine how he could have overlooked such a courtesy, and "The next evening Balanchine sent me one hundred roses, delivered on stage in an enormous bouquet. There were so many I couldn't carry them all home." This anecdote reflects both Balanchine's generosity and his failure of attention to anything that didn't seem important to him.

In 1928 and 1929 came the two great Balanchine/Diaghilev works that have survived, recognized everywhere as masterpieces. *Apollon Musagète* (now *Apollo*) was the first of the true collaborations with Stravinsky, the ballet that Balanchine was to call the turning point of his life. The score, for string orchestra, evoked a different world from that of the big orchestral statements of *Firebird, Petrouchka,* and *Le Sacre.* It radiated harmony, quiet certitude. Balanchine at once understood both its greatness and its possibilities for him. He has explained how its stripped-

away language gave him the courage to eliminate the unnecessary from his own work—"to dare to not use all my ideas." It also helped him grasp that a given ballet must have a vocabulary of its own, steps and gestures that all inhabit a single universe.

Apollo, Leader of the Muses is an account of the birth of the god (at first he's an unlicked cub) and his exposure to three of the nine muses—Calliope, muse of poetry; Polyhymnia, muse of mime; and Terpsichore, muse of dance. He lays aside his lyre, seats himself on a simple stool, and requires each of them to reveal herself to him. After their three solos, interrupted by his own, he chooses Terpsichore (of course) as his personal muse. Now, having achieved godhead, he can ascend with the three demigoddesses to Parnassus.

Apollo's daring marriage of classicism and modernism made it the crucial work of neoclassicism in dance, leading not only to the immense body of Balanchine's future work but to so much else in twentieth-century ballet. At the time, however, no one could have guessed how influential it would be, although the composer Nicolas Nabokov reports having heard Diaghilev, at a rehearsal, turn to André Derain and say, "What he is doing is magnificent. It is pure classicism, such as we have not seen since Petipa's." Even so, after the triumphant Paris premiere, with Stravinsky conducting, it was Lifar's leg that Diaghilev stooped to kiss; he had done such a thing only once before, with Nijinsky after the first performance of *Spectre de la rose*. As Taper wryly remarks, "Nobody offered to kiss the choreographer's leg."

The circumstances of *Apollo*'s creation were not as harmonious as the ballet itself. Balanchine had made the role of Terpsichore

on Danilova, but Lord Rothermere had demanded that his "protégée," Alice Nikitina, a lesser dancer, be given an important premiere in Paris, so Danilova was replaced. Then Terpsichore's solo wasn't exactly right by opening night, and in one of his rare misjudgments, Diaghilev insisted that it was boring and had to be dropped. Balanchine and Stravinsky were angry, and there was a quarrel, Balanchine announcing that the problem wasn't with the solo but with Nikitina. Nonetheless, the solo was eliminated on the second night, then immediately restored, Balanchine having made some adjustments to it. From then on Nikitina and Danilova alternated in the role, and Danilova was awarded the London premiere. ("Besides, I reasoned, London was as important a city for ballet as Paris.") Balanchine was upset by what had happened, she says, but typically never said anything to her about it—these two, remember, were living together as man and wife. There was also a problem with the awkward costumes, which were soon replaced by simple Grecian tunics made (out of tricot) by Diaghilev's great friend Chanel.

Apollo had been created in record time—"the steps just poured from him," Danilova reports. But at first they weren't easy for the dancers to master: "We were the first ones to interpret Balanchine's movements, to find that path. The steps were very difficult to perform. It was for the second generation to take what we had done and build on it . . . we had a hard enough time grasping that new style and finding a way to express it. On opening night, we all felt the excitement of being in on something new . . . we knew that we had done something great."

The greatness of *Apollo* has survived, but the ballet has under-

gone radical changes since 1928. It shed its original "primitive" set and costumes, its chariot, Apollo's laurel wreath; then, in the seventies, Balanchine dropped the birth scene and reworked the ending, eliminating the final ascension up a set of stairs toward the sun. At different times he also adjusted certain steps, as when Suzanne Farrell took over the role of Terpsichore. Even so, *Apollo* is instantly recognizable, filled with unforgettable moments and passages and intensely moving, as we respond to the story of the education of a god, the growth of a boy into a man. And it has a special and profound resonance for all who love dance, for Apollo's choice of Terpsichore is an homage to dance itself.

Late in 1928 came a slight but highly successful work, *The Gods Go a-Begging,* with music by Handel orchestrated by Thomas Beecham, who conducted (and whose extremely wealthy father had been one of Diaghilev's most loyal sponsors). It featured Danilova, and Balanchine put it together in about a week during the 1928 London season. And then, in 1929, came *The Prodigal Son,* to a score commissioned from Prokofiev and with sets by Rouault, who took so long finishing them that the sketches had to be snatched from his hands. This retelling of the biblical parable was both startling in itself and startling in that it suggested a new commitment by Diaghilev to serious dance-drama. It was, of course, like *Apollo,* to feature Lifar, who was still the reigning favorite, although Grigoriev tells us that Diaghilev had turned "positively cold" to Lifar, whom he now considered to be "sly and scheming, too ambitious and too fond of self-advertisement."

Perhaps there was something in the story itself that appealed to Diaghilev—the young man crawling (literally) back to his father in abject guilt and remorse. In his eyes, Nijinsky had betrayed him, Massine had betrayed him (he, too, had dared to marry), and Balanchine was showing signs of independence. The message: prodigal sons, beware. In this work, Balanchine managed to reveal intense sympathy not only for the foolish Prodigal, who is stripped of his pride, his worldly possessions, even his clothes by the seductive and heartless Siren, but for the stern patriarch as well. The ingenuity of the action, the startling *pas de deux* with the Siren (John Taras, Balanchine's longtime colleague, has described it as "a manual of erotic combinations"), the depth of feeling conveyed—all these elements separate *Prodigal Son* from the dramatics, or melodramatics, of earlier dance-dramas like *Schéhérazade*. Lifar had another tremendous success in *Prodigal*, as did Doubrovska as the Siren—she says that when Diaghilev and Balanchine told her to go home and think about her part, she decided to approach it like a snake, without any feeling. The greatest Sirens of the future were all to have this cold, inhuman aspect.

Balanchine would revive *Prodigal Son* several times—for Jerome Robbins, and later for Edward Villella, whose signature role it became. He also taught it to Mikhail Baryshnikov. But Taper reports Balanchine telling him that Lifar was the most exciting of all the Prodigals, just as he was the most impressive Apollo—not surprisingly, since these roles were made for him, to reflect his highly specialized qualities. On the other hand, more than forty-five years after the creation of *Prodigal Son*, when

Baryshnikov was joining New York City Ballet and I asked Balanchine whether he was making a new ballet for him (at that time I was programming the company's seasons and needed to know), he replied sharply, "Diaghilev made me make ballets for Lifar. I never do that again. Misha very useful dancer, can do anything. We don't treat him like star." In other words, no matter how much he appreciated Baryshnikov's genius, having had to obey Diaghilev's commands still rankled, and at New York City Ballet the choreographer was the star.

Whatever resentment Balanchine may have felt toward Diaghilev in this regard, he also acknowledged that Diaghilev was the deciding factor in his artistic life, the man who identified his talent, educated him, polished him, granted him extraordinary opportunities. "It is because of Diaghilev," he was to say, "that I am whatever I am today." In the summer of 1929, Diaghilev, whose health had grown increasingly unstable, died suddenly, in Venice, of diabetes. The loss to the Ballets Russes was incalculable. The shock was overwhelming. In Paris the steady, unemotional Grigoriev received a telegram saying, DIAGHILEV DIED THIS MORNING. INFORM COMPANY. LIFAR. He writes, "I read this terrible telegram over and over again. I could not take it in. Diaghilev dead! The idea seemed nonsensical. And then, as the truth was borne in on me, I grew dizzy, and for the first time in my life I fainted."

As for Balanchine, he was in a film studio in London, preparing to shoot a dance sequence with Lydia Lopokova (the wife of the economist John Maynard Keynes) and Anton Dolin for a movie called *Dark Red Roses,* England's first sound film. A

newsboy came by and Dolin spotted a picture of Diaghilev on the front page. Crying *"Serge Pavlovitch est mort!"* he rushed back to the others with the awful news.

It was news that would permanently alter the configuration of the dance world, creating a diaspora of talent that would struggle for years to relocate itself in some kind of permanence. For Balanchine it would mean four years of wandering—if not in the wilderness, then in uncertainty and anxiety. His fate was to create dances, but creating dances requires stable institutions, and there were very few of those in the world at that time.

As a Dancer

Above left: With Tamara Geva in *Étude*

Above right: As Kastchei in *Firebird*

Left: With Tamara Toumanova (on stool) and Natalie Strakhova in *Cotillon*

Right: With Felia Doubrovska in *Le Bal*

Chapter Three

On His Own

Of all the ballet companies in the West, by far the biggest and most prestigious was the Paris Opéra Ballet. A few months after Diaghilev's death, in 1929, its chief administrator, Jacques Rouché, invited Balanchine to stage a new two-act ballet to Beethoven's *Les Créatures de Promethée*, an invitation he accepted at once, despite what must have been misgivings about the Opéra's notorious politicking and backbiting. It was also suggested to him that he would be made the company's *maître de ballet*. But soon after beginning work on this new commission, he fell ill. His health had never been strong, and now he was struck down by a virulent pneumonia—so serious that at one point his life was in danger. The pneumonia led to pleurisy. During this tense period, it became clear that he could not finish the ballet for the Opéra, which was to have featured Lifar. And it was Lifar whom Balanchine recommended to complete the job, although he had almost no experience as a choreographer.

Every day Lifar and his colleagues would come to Balanchine's bedroom and receive advice and instructions as to how to

proceed. "Do you think I can do it, George?" Lifar kept asking, and George kept reassuring him. By the time the pleurisy had turned into tuberculosis, Lifar was able to continue on his own, and it was under his sole authorship that *Les Créatures de Prométhée* was eventually premiered. Meanwhile, Balanchine was ordered to a sanatorium, and Danilova installed him in a hospital in Passy in the French Alps of the Haute-Savoie. There he stayed, alone, feverish, and weak. The doctors decided to remove one lung, but he absolutely refused; the knee operation two years earlier had been a disaster, and he felt he needed a full recovery to continue as a choreographer. As was so often the case throughout his life, he left it to fate to decide what would become of him.

The sanatorium insisted on an exacting regimen that he found antipathetic. "My life here is not gay," he wrote to Boris Kochno, "and the only good thing about it is my hope—that is, my hope of seeing my old friends around the 6th when they come here for a rest. Obviously, they are not going to find much gaiety waiting for them, but rest they can. We sleep a lot, and the food comes out of our ears." The guests did not come, but he did recover, and on his own terms. After three months he was well enough to return to Paris and resume his life. But surely the experience marked him. Years later he said to the dancer Ruthanna Boris, "You know, I am really a dead man. I was supposed to die and I didn't, and so now everything I do is second chance."

Back in Paris, Balanchine went with Danilova to the Opéra to see a performance of *Prométhée,* which was having a consider-

able success. When they tried to go backstage to congratulate Lifar, they were denied entrance. According to Danilova, George told the doorkeeper, "Well, there must be some mistake," and sent Lifar a message. The answer came back: "Mr. Lifar does not wish to see Mr. Balanchine." Bernard Taper omits this story—Balanchine must either have denied it or chosen to forget it during the long incubation period of Taper's biography. Instead, Taper describes a meeting during which Balanchine congratulates Lifar on his success and also mentions that he will probably pursue that ballet-master job at the Opéra. Lifar is discouraging about it, and no wonder—some days later it's announced that the Opéra's new *maître de ballet* is to be Serge Lifar.

With the door closed on the Paris Opéra—and probably a good thing, too, given the Byzantine nature of that institution—Balanchine immediately left for London. He had been hired by the successful theatrical producer C. B. Cochran to stage the dance numbers for the *Cochran Review* of 1930. Adapting at once to the constrictions of the small Pavillion Theatre and to the chic atmosphere of the Cochran shows, he devised a series of small, sophisticated dances or sketches that perfectly suited the occasion. Perhaps the most impressive of these was *Luna Park,* with music by Lord Berners and a libretto by Kochno, about sideshow freaks, one of whom was Lord Rothermere's Nikitina (in her memoirs she asserts that it was she who alerted Cochran to Balanchine), who appeared with only a single leg. Efimov was on hand, too (he had two heads), and—despite whatever resent-

ment might have existed between the two men—so was Lifar, to whom Balanchine gave two extra pairs of arms. It was all a tremendous success.

From London he was off to Copenhagen, where he had been engaged as a guest ballet master for the Royal Danes. The Danes thought they wanted something new, but Balanchine's new was *too* new; he understood that what they really wanted was some of the Diaghilev/Fokine/Massine standards—*Schéhérazade, The Three-Cornered Hat, La Boutique fantasque.* As always, he was obliging, and the only works of his own that he staged in Denmark were *Apollo,* which the Danes liked, and *Barabau,* which they didn't. This was when he performed *Spectre* with Ulla Poulsen at a charity matinee, and she reports that he also took the male role in *Les Sylphides*—the only time he ever danced it, and, she says, he danced it "very beautifully." She also remarks on his wisdom in concentrating on ballets with strong mime and emotional content rather than the high-classical style of the Maryinsky-trained Russians. She herself treasured the entire experience, conceding that "The only thing I couldn't do was a real Balanchine ballet, because I had weak feet." But the consensus was that the experiment had been a failure, both for the company and Balanchine. In a letter to Kochno he wrote, "The people here are shit. Nobody understands anything. Their heads are empty unless they see something resembling a sandwich." In any case, there could be no permanent place for a Balanchine in a dance world centered on the delicate, domestic style of the ballets of August Bournonville.

From Copenhagen he brought Danilova in Paris a present of lapis lazuli earrings. She was disappointed: "I had been expecting diamonds, so I threw the earrings in his face." She also used him as target practice for a bottle of cheap perfume he had presented her with. Worst of all, he had shipped a snazzy new green car from Denmark, and she had outfitted herself to match its color, but there was a problem with import duties, and according to legend, he solved the problem by simply giving the car to a total stranger there on the dock. Another disappointment for Danilova.

Now it was back to London and to further work in revue, this time for impresario Sir Oswald Stoll at the Coliseum ("SIXTEEN DELIGHTFUL BALANCHINE GIRLS SIXTEEN"). He was well paid but not very interested—except in living in London, which he always enjoyed. He had elegant suits made, learned to roll an umbrella, even went riding in Hyde Park. But when his work for Stoll was done, he couldn't stay on in England—not even the influence of John Maynard Keynes could procure him the necessary papers—so back he went to Paris. And Danilova.

It's unclear from the various accounts on just which return home the lapis lazuli crisis took place, but it *is* clear that the Balanchine-Danilova relationship had run its course. They were hardly ever in the same city at the same time, they no longer worked together inside a stable company—which meant that he could no longer choreograph ballets on her—and their temperaments didn't match. Danilova was practical about money, hard-headed, ambitious; Balanchine was indifferent to money, uncalculating, passive.

Nor did their life together seem based on passion. It was more of a working friendship, with not much heart involved. By the time she was throwing things at him, they were more like *commedia dell'arte* figures than serious lovers or man and wife. She took a job in a musical comedy in London and wrote him a letter suggesting it would be better for them both if they were free. "For a long time there was no answer from him. And then finally a letter came saying that if I wanted to leave him, I should do exactly as I pleased. That was all." She claims that she still loved him and missed him, but neither of them had been exactly monogamous, and it seems likely that any regrets they had soon passed.

As was to be expected, various members of the Diaghilev diaspora began to regroup in an attempt to continue his work—and theirs. The most logical place to begin was in Monte Carlo, where the company had spent so many years, where the opera season still required dancers and dance makers, and where there was an established audience for ballet. The talented René Blum, brother of the famous Socialist politician Léon Blum, was director of the new Ballets Russes, and Blum invited Balanchine to be guest *maître de ballet* for a four-month period beginning in January 1932, with that other old Diaghilev hand Boris Kochno to collaborate as *"conseiller artistique."* Naturally, Danilova expected to be asked to come along, but Balanchine informed her that she didn't fit in with his plans: Everybody was to be young, young, young, and "Frankly, you're just too old." Choura, twenty-eight, was not pleased. (The last word, however, was to be hers. Balan-

chine would choreograph on her again in the forties—*Danses Concertantes, Night Shadow, Song of Norway*—and choreograph *with* her several times: *Raymonda,* in 1946, for the Ballets Russes and, most important, *Coppélia,* in 1974, for New York City Ballet. And she would teach at the School of American Ballet for decades until her retirement in 1989, half a dozen years after Balanchine's death. She had known him earliest, longest, and possibly, given the shrewdness of her remarks about him, best.)

Balanchine was far from wanting to follow in Diaghilev's footsteps. He would even have preferred to eliminate the word "Russes" from the company's name, but that label had far too much drawing power throughout Europe to be discarded, and "Ballets Russes de Monte Carlo" was the name eventually decided upon by management. Balanchine did not arrive in Monte Carlo empty handed. In Paris he had discovered three very young girls with amazing technical proficiency: Tamara Toumanova, Irina Baronova, and Tatiana Riabouchinska, who were variously known to be twelve, thirteen, fourteen, or fifteen—take your pick. (The English dancer Diana Gould [later Menuhin], who was in the company, was to comment, "I can't remember how many times we celebrated Toumanova's fifteenth birthday.") These were the famous "baby ballerinas" who, with Danilova and Markova, were to dominate ballet in the West well into the forties. Two of them had been trained by the great Maryinsky star Olga Preobrajenska, one by the even greater Maryinsky star Mathilda Kschesinskaya—the two émigré ladies remained an important force in the ballet world for many years.

The three girls were different in appearance and temperament. Toumanova was pale-faced and raven-haired, glamorous, and, in the photographs, more mature looking than her years. She also reveled in displaying her astounding, implacable *fouettés*. Baronova was charming and appealing and a formidable classicist. Riabouchinska had wonderful ingenuous dash and style. They had several things in common beside their superb training: They all had fiercely protective (and competitive) "mamas," and they all adored Balanchine. As Kathrine Sorley Walker put it in her invaluable history of the company, "They all fell in love with him, as girls at a finishing school might universally fall for a good-looking music master."

During his few months at Monte Carlo, Balanchine would create ballets for almost twenty operas, from *La Périchole* to *Le Prophète*. But of chief concern to him were the two new ballets he was making, *La Concurrence* and *Cotillon*. The first was a lighthearted tale of two rival tailors, their competing wives, and their customers. With its bright costumes and decor by Derain and its pleasing score by Auric, it stayed in the company's repertory for years. *Cotillon,* with its brilliant Chabrier score, was something more—of all Balanchine's "lost" ballets, the one most mourned by those who knew it. (A recent attempt at reconstruction hasn't restored it to the general repertory.)

A young girl is preparing for a ball. The guests arrive, and are greeted by the Master of the Cotillion. There is an entertainment—dances by harlequins, jockeys, Spaniards. Then a mysterious duet—"The Hand of Fate"—followed by a fortune-telling sequence and then a thrilling finale as the Girl performs count-

less *fouettés* while the guests swirl around her. The Girl was Toumanova, and it was with this sequence that, in Sorley Walker's words, she "moved into the memories of a generation." From the first, *Cotillon* cast a spell over audiences and critics alike. "The aura of the fatal ballroom," wrote the critic A. V. Coton, "the loveliness of corruption, the sense of sweet sin implicit in every move and gesture is the triumph of atmosphere." And "atmosphere" is the word most closely associated with this ballet. The brief film clips that exist suggest this quality, but I suspect we can better infer it from Balanchine's 1951 *La Valse,* which Coton's words eerily anticipate.

The honeymoon between Balanchine and Monte Carlo was quickly over, and soon he was gone. Accounts differ as to why. The most dramatic is that Léon Blum's somewhat sinister associate Colonel Wassily de Basil (who would ruthlessly take over the company) simply hired Massine in his place, without bothering to inform Balanchine that he had done so. And Balanchine was known to have described de Basil as "an octopus. A crooked octopus, and with bad taste." It is also possible that Balanchine and Kochno simply had had enough of de Basil. Kathrine Sorley Walker sensibly suggests that nobody fired anybody and nobody quit; that when the four-month contract lapsed, it just wasn't renewed. In any case Balanchine, as always, was ready and eager for the next step.

He and Kochno were back in Paris, already discussing new ballets, even though they had no company, no backer, and no money. They did have Toumanova, who insisted on following

Balanchine, as well as a few other dancers from the Monte Carlo troupe. In the spirit of Mr. Micawber, Balanchine was certain that something would turn up, and something did—a rich young Englishman named Edward James, who thought it might help his marriage to the headstrong Viennese dancer and actress Tilly Losch if he made her a gift of a ballet company. As Taper reminds us, "A ballet company as a present for one's loved one is a more princely gift than a diamond necklace from Cartier's." (It failed to do the trick: James and Losch would soon be embroiled in a scandalous divorce suit. But not until he had spent a million or so francs on Balanchine's Les Ballets 1933.)

Losch was an effective performer with limited technique. Balanchine made the best of things, quickly staging three pieces for her, two of which were of consequence. *L'Errante,* set to Schubert's "The Wanderer Fantasy," had lighting, "dramatic effects," and costumes by Pavel Tchelitchev (except for the dress Molyneux designed for Losch). Photographs and reviews suggest that it was highly atmospheric—dark shadows and diffused light—and highly sculptural (not too much difficult movement for Losch beyond managing her ten-yard train). Agnes de Mille, in her more acerbic mode, wrote "Such was Balanchine's genius that she seemed to be dancing on the beat. But try as he might he couldn't make her emotionally moving." Nor was de Mille impressed by the equally ambitious *Les Sept Péchés Capitaux (The Seven Deadly Sins),* with its score by Kurt Weill and text by Bertolt Brecht, and its doppelgänger Annas—Tilly Losch dancing and Lotte Lenya singing.

Three of the six ballets Balanchine staged in record time for

Les Ballets 1933 were for the faithful Toumanova, one of them to a score that held his attention through his entire life: Tchaikovsky's *Mozartiana*. Toumanova remembered that Christian "Bébé" Berard "dressed me in a black tutu, up to the top of the knee. There were ostrich feathers in the hat. I represented a magnificent racehorse, proud, without putting the nose up, but with that look of nobility, pride with technique. This is what Balanchine gave me. There was no chichi. It was elegant, strong, magnificent, without any smiles. . . . Everything was with dignity, but fast, exciting, alive." (De Mille thought it "very thin," but she was overwhelmed by Toumanova: "I sat there and wept.") *Mozartiana* was a major effort, but although Paris embraced the company as a fashionable event, the ballets themselves did not fare particularly well. And they were even less appreciated in London when the company opened there in the summer of '33— to the overwhelming competition of the de Basil Ballets Russes. Soon, the James-Balanchine company collapsed in a welter of hysteria, recriminations, and lawsuits.

With Les Ballets 1933, Balanchine had indicated the adventurous path he hoped to follow, but there seemed to be little possibility of his doing so in the immediate future. What few opportunities suggested themselves would not offer him the independence he required in order to fulfill his large artistic ambitions. But as usual he did nothing to plot his course: Fate would take a hand. And, of course, it did—in the form of a young American who was in love with ballet and had come to Europe in search of a choreographer of genius whom he could persuade to come to the United States and launch a classical ballet company.

. . .

Lincoln Kirstein was the son of one of the owners of Filene's department store in Boston, and his parents encouraged him in— or at least failed to *dis*courage him from—a life of service to the arts. As a Harvard undergraduate, he had helped found the Harvard Society for Contempory Art, a forerunner of New York's Museum of Modern Art; he had published a collection of poems and a novel; and he had co-founded and edited an influential literary magazine, *Hound & Horn,* that published Ezra Pound, T. S. Eliot, Hart Crane, and printed Kirstein's own tribute to Diaghilev. When he realized that he was not equipped to be a dancer, Kirstein determined to emulate Diaghilev, of whom he was to write, "He created a taste in and of his own period, he set up the only referable standards of aesthetic excellence in the first quarter of the twentieth century and provided the only great market for a unified creative endeavor." Obsessed with Nijinsky, at home (through his formidable sister, Mina, who was living in England) with the Bloomsbury set and its connections to the world of Diaghilev, he had accidentally, in the summer of 1929, stumbled upon Diaghilev's funeral cortege in Venice: an omen if ever there was one. Now, in 1933, he was prepared to make his move.

On his annual trips to Europe, he had been struck by *Apollo, Prodigal Son, La Chatte*—the finest fruits of Balanchine's Diaghilev period. He had just seen what Balanchine had accomplished for Les Ballets 1933. And he had heard from various advisers, including Tchelitchev, that the young Balanchine was the most talented, most individual balletmaster anywhere. Tchelitchev:

"My dee-ar boy; if you want to make ballet—take Balanchine. Only possible with him. No one else—now." Besides, he was probably available. Why would the established Massine abandon the Ballets Russes or Lifar the Paris Opéra for such a hare-brained scheme?

Kirstein had been working with Romola Nijinsky on her biography of her husband, and it was through Romola that he first encountered Balanchine, at a performance of Les Ballets 33 at the Savoy Theatre in London. ("Balanchine came out looking haggard and tired.") But it was the following week, on July 11, that Balanchine and Kirstein began to talk, in the kitchen of their friend in common, the American art dealer Kirk Askew. "Balanchine seemed intense, concentrated, disinterested," Kirstein wrote in his diary, "not desperate, exactly, but without any hope. I like to imagine we got on well; he said nothing about meeting again." He did, however, remark that American students "have spirit and can be touched into fire." Within the week, the diary reports, "Balanchine says America has always been his dream, even before he left Russia; he is now willing to risk everything for it." Kirstein waited in suspense before Balanchine agreed, on July 16, to take the risk. Kirstein's offer must have seemed to him both a lifeline and a fantasy come true. But he was cautious. Proper arrangements had to be agreed upon.

Kirstein had two partners-in-waiting back in America. One was his Harvard classmate Edward Warburg, of the very rich banking family, whom he had talked into taking his plans seriously and who was prepared to put up money to carry them out.

The other was another Harvard friend, A. Everett "Chick" Austin, who was now the director of the Wadsworth Atheneum in Hartford, Connecticut, where the projected new school was to be located. It was after his long meeting with Balanchine on July 16 that Kirstein wrote his famous letter to Chick Austin: "This will be the most important letter I will ever write to you. . . . My pen burns in my hand as I write. . . . We have a real chance to have an American ballet within 3 years time. . . . I won't be able to hear from you for a week—but I won't sleep until I do. Just say *Proceed* or *Impossible*. . . . We have the future in our hands." On July 26 the reply came, and its message was to proceed. On August 6, Austin announced that some money had been pledged toward the enterprise. Two days later, he telegraphed again: "Go ahead; ironclad contract necessary, beginning October 15. Settle as much as possible now. Bring photos, publicity. Museum willing; can't wait. Chick."

A few days after that, Kirstein was in Paris, meeting with Balanchine and Vladimir Dimitriev to sweat out the arrangements. On August 11 the three men got down to specifics, with Dimitriev laying down the law. Since leading Balanchine, Danilova, and the others out of Bolshevik Russia, Dimitriev had stood by, handling practical matters for them and sharing in their income. In the discussions now, two things were insisted upon: In America, they must start with a school, with the company to follow, and Dimitriev's presence was nonnegotiable. It was understood that he would accompany Balanchine to the United States, and so, they believed, would Toumanova and Mama

Toumanova, as well as some other dancers. Kirstein agreed to all this, and immediately set out for America to prepare the way. Richard Buckle reprints the frantic cables between Kirstein and Balanchine on Kirstein's arrival back home late in August:

August 29, GB to LK: "Await your decision. Presence Dmitriew is necessary." The same day, LK to GB: "Sure complete success. Minor difficulties cleared by September 15th. . . . Great enthusiasm." "Minor difficulties" included money, visas, and the involuntary defection of Toumanova, who had been misled by de Basil about Balanchine's plans and tricked into rejoining the Ballets Russes (or else her mother had thought better of the American plan). Kirstein's determination and energy, and the steady support of his friends, prevailed, and by October 10 everything had been arranged. GB to LK: "Sailing Olympic. Would be very much obliged if communicate Tamara Geva our arrival."

At the age of twenty-nine, nine years after arriving in the West, Balanchine was on his way to a new world and a new life, his only connections the twenty-six-year-old Lincoln Kirstein, whom he barely knew, and an ex-wife he hadn't seen in half a dozen years.

Chapter Four

To America

On October 18, 1933, the *Olympic* docked in New York with Balanchine and Dimitriev on board. They were met by Kirstein and Warburg, who were eager to show them the town, and anxious that they like it. Serious discussions began at once about the school (to be called the School of American Ballet, reflecting Balanchine's determination that it was *American* ballet he had come to teach). Two crises arose immediately. Hartford, Connecticut, was hardly a fit successor to St. Petersburg, Paris, London, and Monte Carlo, and it wasn't long before Balanchine decided he would not set up his school—and his life—there. This proved a bitter pill for Chick Austin, who had been instrumental in helping Kirstein get Balanchine to America. And then Balanchine fell badly ill, and for a month or so was nursed back to health by Kirstein's sister, Mina Curtiss; the cure, apparently, involved eating great amounts of eggs, butter, and cream, a diet on which he gained thirty pounds in thirty days. Even so, the doctors were certain that he had only a few more years to live.

With Hartford a thing of the past, a new location was found for the school in Manhattan, at Madison Avenue and Fifty-

ninth Street, in a studio that had once been Isadora Duncan's. There had been some advance notice of the school's official opening date of January 2, 1934, and by the end of December a number of pupils were enrolled. The faculty comprised Balanchine, Pierre Vladimirov (a superb dancer who had been Pavlova's partner and a *premier danseur* at the Maryinsky), and Dorothy Littlefield, a young dancer and teacher from Philadelphia. The management consisted of Dimitriev, commander in chief, who considered Kirstein and Warburg complete amateurs (which they were); Warburg, in charge of financial matters; and Kirstein, in charge of propaganda, a favorite role of his.

Quickly more students began to arrive. The roll call in the first six months includes many of the dancers who would become associated with Balanchine over the next ten years: among others, William Dollar, Lew and Harold Christensen, Marie-Jeanne (Palus), Gisella Caccialanza, Ruthanna Boris, Annabelle Lyon. These are the dancers he would use because these were the dancers he was training according to his theories and preferences. There were already capable dancers in America, some trained by Fokine, who had a successful studio in New York, others by ex-dancers who had dropped out along the way from Pavlova and Diaghilev touring companies and set up schools of their own. But these dancers didn't dance the way Balanchine wanted them to, and had to be retrained. That was why he felt there had to be a school first—so that he could manufacture the basic material from which he could then make the kind of ballets he wanted to make.

In retrospect it seems fortunate that Toumanova and other Ballets Russes dancers didn't come with him to New York. They

were far more polished than those he was starting out with, but he had no intention of imitating the repertory or the style of the Ballets Russes. Again, this was the School of *American* Ballet, just as the first company he and Kirstein assembled would be the *American* Ballet. American young girls, Kirstein has written,

> were not sylphides; they were basketball champions and queens of the tennis court, whose proper domain was athletics. They were long-legged, long-necked, slim-hipped, and capable of endless acrobatic virtuosity. The drum majorettes, the cheer-leader of the high-school football team of the thirties filled [Balanchine's] eye. . . . The pathos and suavity of the dying swan, the purity and regal behavior of the elder ballerina, were to be replaced by a raciness, an alert celerity which claimed as its own the gaiety of sport and the skill of the champion athlete.

In order to have something to teach the students with—something they could handle yet would stretch their abilities—he began, in March 1934, to choreograph a new ballet on them. This was *Serenade*, which would become what is probably his most loved original work. There are famous stories of the birth of *Serenade*: How it was composed for seventeen girls because that's how many were available the day he started; how he incorporated into its action a girl who came in late one day (Annabelle Lyon), and another girl who fell down (Heidi Vossler). Ruthanna Boris was there that first day of the creation of *Serenade*, and in her as-yet-unpublished memoir remembers how, after class one day, Balanchine announced, "Take rest . . . we will make some steps."

Everyone knew what that meant: "We, his chosen American dancers, were about to begin work on a new choreography made on US! The American Ballet was about to happen!"

First he escorted each girl into the center of the studio, carefully placing her in the design he was making. "A picture emerged. . . . It was totally unlike any group placement I had ever seen—the usual, a faceless set of straight lines dancing behind a soloist. Mr. George Balanchine was making lines where everyone could be seen!"

Every day he spent two or three hours working on *Serenade*. Boris, who came from the very different world of opera-ballet at the Metropolitan, was fascinated by the process. She herself would become a distinguished choreographer, and her eye was that of a choreographer in the making.

> Mr. Balanchine did not model his steps clearly, carefully, or technically—he indicated them, moved through them fleetingly, often giving body and arm positions by name at the same time. He ran, jumped, turned, changed direction, made combinations of classroom steps that looked like improvisation instead of technical practice. He gave positions following swiftly after each other that blended one into the next—he often looked like a kaleidoscope—fluid, flexible, free. He went all the way down to the floor and then bounded up into the air—he kneeled, stretched up to standing, wove our arms and torsos in and out of linkings with each other. As I watched him darting among his dancers, placing arms, tilting heads, curving torsos, he made me think

of a bee among flowers—he looked serious and happy at the same time. When he was pleased with a result of his exertions he giggled his dry little giggle. We became participants in the process—he shared his pleasure when making dances with all of us. There were times his combinations seemed to surprise him—he asked "You can do like this? You say to me if is comfortable, not comfortable"—"You must say to me about if you can do *en pointe*. I am man—I do not go *en pointe*." I felt he trusted us—loved working with us—wanted us to have as much to do with what he made for us as he did. Rehearsing with Mr. George Balanchine, day after day, became a never-ending discovery of new ways to dance.

This is what Balanchine was like at work when he was thirty, on the occasion of his first creative work in America, but it reflects many of his lifelong practices: swift invention that seemed almost impromptu; consideration for the comfort of his dancers and respect for their abilities; sureness; joy in demonstration. "The speed and craft with which he works are astounding," wrote Paul Taylor decades later; "the rehearsal time being used economically, none of it taken up by explanation of concepts, poetic imagery, or motivation." The composer Elliott Carter, who would often go to the Fifty-ninth Street studio to watch rehearsals, wrote, "When you saw Balanchine indicating the dance, showing the choreography to his dancers, it seems as though he was just inventing things moment by moment, as if there was no plan for anything, as if he was improvising. . . . But then when it actually happened onstage the ballet didn't seem like that at all, you saw the whole thing he

had in his mind." Martha Graham, at the time of their joint venture, *Episodes,* described the process more poetically (as reported by Taper): "It's like watching light pass through a prism. The music passes through him, and in the same natural yet marvelous way that a prism refracts light, he refracts music into dance."

By June *Serenade* was finished, although in later years Balanchine would expand and revise it. Even its style was to change: Marie-Jeanne remembers that whereas later it became "Fokiney"— and, indeed, it's often thought of as Balanchine's *Les Sylphides*— back then it was "very sharp, very precise." Eddie Warburg asked his parents to give him as a twenty-sixth birthday present the opportunity to stage an outdoor performance of *Serenade* and two other ballets on their estate near White Plains. Despite the absence of an orchestra (there was a piano in the bushes), and the deficiencies of the students, and rain, and Dimitriev making scenes in the great Russian tradition, the performance took place—*Serenade,* and two pieces from Les Ballets 1933, *Mozartiana* and *Les Songes.* The Warburgs' lawn "never recovered from the shock."

It was six months before the first public performance, at the forgiving Chick Austin's theater in Hartford, which proved to be an uncongenial ballet venue. Nor was the performance very good. In addition to *Serenade* it featured two other new works: *Alma Mater,* a college football romp—the villain in a coonskin coat—with music by George Gershwin's friend Kay Swift, and costumes by the famous cartoonist John Held Jr., and with a libretto by Eddie Warburg himself (he was chagrined when Balanchine refused to attend a real football game); and *Transcendence,* a romantic ballet to Lizst, with a Kirstein libretto.

This was the first time the company assumed its name: the American Ballet. Both the name and the fact that one of these ballets had a popular American theme reflected the current interest in Americana. One of the crosses Balanchine and Kirstein had to bear was that the only dance critic in the country of any consequence, John Martin of the *New York Times,* was strongly opposed to their venture because he thought Balanchine was too European, too Russian, not American. The best thing the American Ballet could do, he was to suggest, was "to get rid of Balanchine and his European notions, and hire a good American dance man."

A two-week season in New York was somehow arranged, and the American Ballet opened at the Adelphi Theater on March 1, 1935, with several programs made up of the inevitable *Serenade, Les Songes* (now known as *Dreams*), *Alma Mater, Transcendence* and, also from Les Ballets 1933, *L'Errante* (now *Errante*), as well as a new potboiler Balanchine whipped up for the tradition-minded, a Russian-type divertissement called *Reminiscence.* Predictably, the last was the piece Martin and the audience preferred. For the pictorial *Errante,* in place of Tilly Losch, Balanchine had Tamara Geva, now remarried and something of a success in New York. She wore Losch's green Molyneux gown and looked wonderful, and according to Ruthanna Boris, she gave all the young American girls in class and the company a fascinating glimpse into the sophistication and glamour of Europe and Balanchine's past.

On the basis of a modest success at the Adelphi, a tour was arranged that was supposed to last fourteen weeks and perform in sixty towns. It opened in October at the Greenwich, Connecticut,

High School, and managed one-night stands in Princeton and Harrisburg before imploding in Scranton, the tour manager having made off with whatever takings there may have been. According to Boris, Balanchine addressed the company: "You know that list you have, tour: we don't have. And bus is outside. Will you please go in bus to New York. Come to class tomorrow, and we will think what to do." But they already knew what they would be doing. To everyone's astonishment, in August the Metropolitan Opera House had extended an invitation to the American Ballet to become its resident dance company. Kirstein was wildly excited: "The vast scale of the Met made me drunk." Balanchine, who had spent too many years making opera-ballets, was less than overwhelmed, but as always he followed where fate beckoned. After all, Kirstein was certain that there would be adventurous ballet nights at the Met—wonderful opportunities for Balanchine to work on that "vast scale," after the humiliations of the Warburg estate, Hartford, and Scranton. As usual, visions of sugarplums danced in Kirstein's head. Balanchine was guardedly optimistic.

From the start, the American Ballet and the Metropolitan Opera did not suit each other. The theater was musty and dusty; there was no time for rehearsal; management was niggardly about costumes and toe shoes; there was a pervasive smell of garlic. Worst of all, the more Balanchine tried to freshen the opera ballets, and the more he succeeded, the less management was pleased—they wanted no distractions from the singers, and they criticized Balanchine for showing no respect for tradition. To which Balanchine rejoined, "Of course not. The tradition of the ballet at the Met is bad ballet." Lew Christensen, who had joined the company, recounted

his experience with Rosa Ponselle, the great soprano, when they were thrown together in *Carmen*. She couldn't be bothered to rehearse with him and, meeting him for the first time on stage, flung a goblet of wine (grapefruit juice) in his face and clamped her mouth to his for at least six seconds. According to Kirstein, during the intermission the Mormon Christensen said, "I thought she was trying to make me in front of God and everybody."

Between the end of 1935 and the summer of 1936, Balanchine created dances for thirteen operas, and occasionally his ballets were scheduled before short operas—*Serenade, Mozartiana, Errante,* or *Reminiscence* would be used to flesh out an evening featuring *Hansel and Gretel,* say. Nobody was happy about what was happening except the dancers, who were being steadily paid. That the company was hired for a second year came as something of a surprise. Perhaps the fact that Eddie Warburg was there to supply funds when needed was an inducement to the Met management.

During Balanchine's stint at the Met, two events of consequence took place. The first was the Met management's startling decision to allow Balanchine to stage Glück's *Orpheus and Eurydice,* with sets and costumes by the avant-garde Tchelitchev. The stage would belong to the dancers; the singers would perform in the orchestra pit. According to Kirstein, the audience "was totally unprepared for an interpretation that transformed vaguely familiar myth and music into a heroicized domestic tragedy of artist, wife, and work; hell as a forced-labor camp; eternity as no happy heaven, but a paradisiacal planetarium where time and space crossed." Indeed, the audience tittered and yawned, and the critics scoffed. But there were those few—

Kirstein among them—who felt that the experiment was a significant achievement. And the Met management, he acknowledges, was "courteously forgiving." *Orpheus and Eurydice* was given two performances and relegated to history.

Of greater consequence was Balanchine's first Stravinsky festival, held at the Met on April 27 and 28, 1937. With money from Warburg, Balanchine was able to commission a new score from Stravinsky, which turned out to be *Jeu de Cartes*. (The ballet was variously called *The Card Party, The Card Game,* and *Poker Game.*) Balanchine's *Apollo* was performed for the first time in America (as *Apollon Musagète*). And for the first time, Balanchine choreographed to *Le Baiser de la Fée (The Fairy's Kiss),* Stravinsky's tribute to Tchaikovsky, which had been commissioned in 1928 by the glamorous (and rich) Ida Rubinstein and choreographed by Nijinska. This was a story and a score Balanchine would return to several times.

The Card Party: A Ballet in Three Deals, costumed and designed by Irene Sharaff, sprang from an idea of Stravinsky's. The Joker keeps interfering with the face cards through three different deals, until he's finally defeated by a royal flush. A witty if brittle piece, it didn't last long when it was revived in 1951 for the New York City Ballet. Decades later, Peter Martins would use the score for a new ballet.

In Lew Christensen, America's finest classical dancer of the time, Balanchine had a noble Apollo. As Kirstein put it, "With Lifar, Balanchine had been given a boy who might conceivably become a young man. In America, with Lew Christensen, he

found a young man who could be credited as a potential divinity." John Martin found that *Apollo* reflected the Diaghilev "period of artiness and affectation"; he didn't like the score, either. (There's no pleasing some people.) Of the three ballets, he much preferred *Le Baiser de la Fée*. But he also wrote that, overall, "The American Ballet covered itself with honor," and even more surprisingly, the two-day enterprise was a popular success.

But this success was not enough to preserve the relationship with the Met, which had frayed beyond repair. It had been an odd marriage to begin with, the modern, vigorous thrust of Balanchine's work at aesthetic odds with the staid ideas and practices of the opera house. Warburg recounts with relish an incident that makes it clear how unsuited Balanchine and the Met were for each other. A German stage director said to him, "Mr. Balanchine, you know Wagner's opera *Rheingold*?" Balanchine, reports Warburg, said "*Da.*" The director went on: "At the Metropolitan the Rhine maidens hang on a trapeze forty feet above the stage and they swim. I want they should be ballet girls. At least one should be black-haired, another brown, and another blond. They must be musical so they know *how* to swim. They must understand German so they know *when* to swim. Above all, Mr. Balanchine, they must not vomit!"

Balanchine went out with a bang, not a whimper. "The Met is a heap of ruins," he told the press, "and every night the stage-hands put it together and make it look a little like opera." He was free both to leave and to express his anger publicly, because by now he had a highly successful, and lucrative, parallel career going: on Broadway and in Hollywood.

AT WORK

Right: With Vera Zorina

Below: With Alexandra Danilova and Frederic Franklin

Opposite: With one of the stars of *The Ballet of the Elephants*

Chapter Five

Broadway and Hollywood

Late in 1935, while he was mounting dances for *Lakmé, La Traviata, Faust,* et al., at the Met, Balanchine was also providing dance numbers for the 1936 edition of the *Ziegfeld Follies,* with music by his old friend Vernon Duke and lyrics by Ira Gershwin. The cast included Bob Hope, Fannie Brice, Eve Arden, Harriet Hocter, the Nicholas Brothers, and—fresh from Paris—Josephine Baker, an old friend from his days there, for whom he concocted something called "Five A.M." ("She had beautiful long legs . . . beautiful," he reminisced years later.) Despite all the exciting elements, the show flopped, but by the time it opened in New York, Balanchine was already working on *Die Meistersinger.*

Two months after that, in April 1936, came the show that put Balanchine squarely on the Broadway map, as well as changing the nature of dance in musical comedy. It was *On Your Toes,* score by Rodgers and Hart, directed by George Abbott, and starring (who else?) Tamara Geva and the great hoofer Ray Bolger (later to become known to the world as the Scarecrow of Oz). This was the first show to integrate dance into its story line,

paving the way for Agnes de Mille's *Oklahoma!*, and (at Balanchine's insistence) the first to credit the dance maker as the "choreographer." And it was a smash hit. The first-act highlight was the parodic *La Princesse Zenobia* ballet—a takeoff on the outmoded orientalisms of *Schéhérazade*. But the real showstopper was the second-act *Slaughter on Tenth Avenue*, in which the hero (Bolger) has to go on hoofing and hoofing and hoofing to avoid being assassinated by a thug hired by a rival *danseur*.

It must have been the participation of Balanchine that inspired Richard Rodgers's irresistible music for *Slaughter,* and Rodgers paid generous tribute to Balanchine's talent and professionalism. To begin with, Rodgers was to say, he was nervous about working with a Russian ballet genius, anticipating all the high drama that the show itself would parody. "I expected fiery temperament. . . . I was scared stiff of him. I asked him . . . did he make the steps and have music written to fit them, or what? He answered, in the thick Russian accent he had then, 'You write, I put on.'" Bolger's testimony is equally telling:

> Balanchine was without a doubt one of the divine characters on this earth, a heavenly person. . . . He was a brilliant brain, quick and humorous and happy when he discovered something. Rodgers's music became to him rather a challenge. He could see the beauty in the theme. He could see a great deal of romance, and he could also see the innocence of my character. So he made a sexy ballet without ever touching. "No touch. Oh, no, no, no touch." I would reach for [Geva's]

breasts, and her hand would come up. Her hand would raise, my hand would reach, and she'd jump . . . "No touch! No touch!" It was really sheer delight.

The two men would go on to work happily together on a "Raffles" ballet in a flop musical called *Keep Off the Grass,* and then again, in 1948, in Frank Loesser's hit *Where's Charley?,* with its showstopping "Once in Love with Amy" number. "This man I adored," Bolger was to say. "Balanchine was the greatest influence in the dance world on my life."

Just a year after *On Your Toes* came Balanchine's second Rodgers and Hart show, *Babes in Arms*—their first to run longer than a year. This time, Balanchine's innovation was a dream ballet, the first in a musical (again anticipating *Oklahoma!*). In an almost unbelievable tour de force, he was working on *Babes in Arms* at exactly the moment he was staging his Stravinsky festival at the Met.

On the strength of the success of *On Your Toes,* Samuel Goldwyn hired Balanchine to come out to Hollywood and create the dance numbers for *The Goldwyn Follies,* its score to be written by George Gershwin. In the spring of 1937, Balanchine and a couple of Russian friends set out for California, which he loved at first sight—the climate, the food markets, the girls. The single note of sorrow came with the sudden death of Gershwin, who had written only five songs for the film before he died and was replaced by Vernon Duke. The inevitable comic mishaps involv-

ing artistic intentions and mixed signals took place between Goldwyn and his new hired hand, but after they got past a dangerous moment when Goldwyn vetoed an elaborate ballet Balanchine had made to *An American in Paris*—his camera techniques were too experimental for the boss—things went well on the set. Off the set, life was more complicated.

A year before, at the opening-night party for *On Your Toes*, Balanchine had met an extraordinarily beautiful dancer whose stage name was Vera Zorina. (Born Brigitta Hartwig, she was always called Brigitta in real life.) The half-German, half-Norwegian Zorina was a soloist with the Ballets Russes, and she had had an intense and disastrous relationship with the much older (and married) Massine. As Zorina put it in her memoirs, when she and George were introduced, "*He* was very nice, *I* was very nice, *it* was very nice." Returning to Europe, she was offered the Geva role in the London production of *On Your Toes*, which, she says, she accepted eagerly because she wanted to dance Balanchine. The show did less well than expected in London, but by then Goldwyn had become interested in her and offered her Hollywood's standard seven-year exclusive contract, her first film to be *The Goldwyn Follies*. She agreed to it, she tells us, only on the condition that Balanchine would be doing the dances.

In the years between his separation from Danilova and his fateful encounter with Zorina in Hollywood there had been many women in Balanchine's life. Although he didn't think he was a handsome man—he described himself to Taper as "rather a shrimp, with a beaky nose and rodent-like front teeth"—many

women found him highly attractive. He had relationships with various women who danced for him, and various lovers and friends have described him as a highly sensual man, but he was hardly a lothario: He courted women one at a time, and was discreet. According to Nathan Milstein, although he was "animated and witty when the conversation was about music," he became more reserved when the topic turned to women. "Handsome and elegant, definitely a ladies' man, he gracefully avoided bragging about his conquests." From what both Geva and Danilova have written about their lives with him, it appears that although he was certainly devoted to them in turn, neither had inspired a burning passion in him. He had not yet given himself totally to another person—perhaps being more or less on his own as a child had trained him in emotional self-sufficiency. He was thirty-two when he met Zorina and the floodgates opened.

His "best platonic woman friend," as she described herself, was Lucia Davidova, who had once been married to Tamara Geva's second husband (it's a small world). She and Balanchine met almost immediately on his arrival in America, and they remained very close until his death fifty years later: At almost any Balanchine event, even in class and rehearsal, she could be seen keeping watch. He confided in her, wept on her shoulder, lived in her house, and she seems to have understood him. "He liked elusiveness in a woman," Davidova would write. "About one of his wives he said, 'I don't need a housewife. I need a nymph who fills the bedroom and floats out. . . .' He always wanted romantic elusiveness. In his ballets the man always seeks and the woman flees. That

is the typical picture of his life." In Zorina he found the quintessential elusive woman—cool, guarded, emotionally unavailable.

Their work together went well. After the aborted *American in Paris* ballet, Balanchine made two large-scale dances for Goldwyn's film. He had brought more than a score of his American Ballet dancers out to Hollywood, and in his first number, William Dollar, one of his leading men, played Romeo to Zorina's Juliet. With his typical witty take on things, Balanchine depicted the Montagues as ballet dancers, the Capulets doing tap. *The Goldwyn Follies,* remember, was being made during the Depression-era populist vs. elite, swing vs. classical wars: Judy Garland vs. Deanna Durbin.

The second, and still famous, dance sequence for *The Goldwyn Follies* was the "Water Nymph" ballet. Before filming began, Balanchine described it to Zorina:

> There will be marvelous, beautiful, big stage, round, with Greek columns on each side like Palladio; then, in the back, statue of big white horse. Poet comes and sees beautiful Undine coming out of pool . . . covered with beautiful white flowers. She slowly, slowly comes out of water—will be *very* sexy with wet material clinging to her body—then she will dance on water, and poet watches and falls in love with her. Then lots of girls appear and they dress her in beautiful ball gown. She dances with poet. Then big storm starts, wind blows like mad, and we discover her on the horse. Then the wind blows all her dress away and she slides slowly, slowly from horse and in her little tunic and bare feet she goes back to lily

pool, and slowly her body disappears in the water until only her head is visible, and then she puts her cheek on the water like a pillow and she is gone like sun disappearing in ocean.

No ballerina could resist such a scenario, and Goldwyn loved it, too. He also developed a crush on Zorina, though throughout the shooting of the movie he kept saying to her, "Zorina, it's got to have warmth." He was right: Warmth is the quality that her screen appearances lack.

Undoubtedly it was her somewhat disdainful manner as well as her elegant beauty and sharp intelligence that drew Balanchine to her. The scenario of the "Water Nymph" ballet is a perfect metaphor for what their relationship was going to become, and variations on it—the enamored man reaching in vain for the unobtainable woman—reappear in Balanchine's work, from *La Sonnambula* to "The Unanswered Question" section of *Ivesiana* to *Meditation* and *Don Quixote*. It can be no accident that he made the latter two for Suzanne Farrell and revived *Sonnambula* and created "The Unanswered Question" for Allegra Kent—two other beautiful girls who proved unattainable.

Zorina was immediately struck by Balanchine's immense competence and sureness as a choreographer, and by his extraordinary command of film technique, although he had been at the studio for only a few weeks. She describes the qualities that so many other dancers have remarked upon:

He was certain what he wanted but sometimes stood still as if listening to inner music and visualizing dance movements.

There was no sign of rapid re-creation of preconceived ideas, but the unfolding of steps and patterns born at that moment from inner impulses. . . . He was calm, he guided people, he never raised his voice or lost his temper. . . . He always seemed to have a solution to a problem and conspiratorially pointed it out, never offending anybody but, rather, producing sighs of relief. The mastery of his craft made him flexible, so that if something didn't work out either in choreography or concepts, he simply changed it.

Richard Rodgers commented on the same phenomenon: "With most other choreographers I've known, it was like asking them to give up some of their living flesh if they were told that, for one reason or another, one of their dance numbers wouldn't work. But Balanchine would just take it in his stride and cheerfully produce on the spot any number of perfectly brilliant ideas to take the place of what came out."

Outside the studio, Zorina and Balanchine became friends, but as he fell in love, she *remained* a friend. There were dinners *à trois*, George and Brigitta's mother, the inevitable Mrs. Hartwig, alternating as cook—cooking was always one of his favorite activities. There were motor trips, long walks. But when Balanchine grew more importunate, Zorina was unable to respond in kind. "I was still raw and wounded, and fearful on a deeper level," she wrote in her autobiography. "My relationship with Massine had been too traumatic, and had made me literally incapable of trusting and giving myself in love to another human

being. I had to mend, to recover, to heal, and to forget—as if it had been a serious illness. This took a long, long time." She felt from the start, though, that she was safe with Balanchine. "I knew George was good, and I felt safe and protected when we were together. . . . I called him my mystical Prince Myshkin and became utterly, completely, and totally devoted to him." Yet she "could not yet return the intensity of his feelings." When early in 1938 he asked her to marry him, she said, "Let's wait." But while she was waiting, she was struck by the attractions of the young Orson Welles, who was equally struck. ("For the first time since Leonide [Massine]," she wrote in her diary, "I found my heart pounding and hands trembling.") As for Balanchine, "George is so tragic, it is almost unbearable."

An immediate outcome of the filming of *Goldwyn Follies* was that Richard Rodgers took one look at Zorina and cast her as the Angel in his upcoming show (with Hart and Balanchine), *I Married an Angel*. It was the perfect American launching pad for Zorina, because, although Balanchine at once began working with her to refine her classical technique, she was never going to be a ballerina on the highest level—a Toumanova, a Danilova— yet, like Geva, she had star quality and large ambitions. *I Married an Angel* made her a star, something she found both intoxicating and unnerving. "Taxi drivers were thrilled to have me in their cabs. Walter Winchell was my biggest fan." But something was missing. "I needed to belong not only to my mother but to my husband. It was time to marry George." And she did. On Christmas Eve 1938, they slipped away to Staten Island and

were secretly married, coming back to Zorina's apartment, where a party was in progress, but not letting on. (His Christmas present to her: an ermine coat, wrapped in a dingy old raincoat—a typical Balanchine practical joke.) The marriage stayed secret until Winchell (of course) spilled the beans.

I Married an Angel eventually closed and went on tour. While it was still running, Balanchine had choreographed another hit Rodgers and Hart musical, *The Boys from Syracuse*—their last together—followed only one week later by Frederick Loewe's first show, *Great Lady*, a flop. Then it was back to Hollywood for the filming of *On Your Toes*. Then back to Broadway for another hit musical, Irving Berlin's *Louisiana Purchase* (Zorina again, costarring William Gaxton, Victor Moore, and Irene Bordoni). Then Hollywood yet again, for *I Was an Adventuress*, with Zorina as a con woman in cahoots with Erich von Stroheim and Peter Lorre but redeemed by Richard Greene. For this one, Balanchine created a surrealist *Swan Lake* sequence that reveals Zorina's lack of classical proficiency, making it all too clear why she would never be a real ballerina. In 1940 came the all-black musical *Cabin in the Sky*, which he directed as well as choreographed (with Katherine Dunham). Starring Ethel Waters, it had songs by Vernon Duke and John Latouche, sets by Boris Aronson, and it featured the terrific song "Taking a Chance on Love," of which Waters had to give something like half a dozen encores on opening night. Although Balanchine was to work on a number of other musicals and operettas, *Cabin in the Sky* remained his most daring and original Broadway venture.

During this period Balanchine was making a great deal of money for the first and only time in his life, and he was spending just about all of it, primarily on a house he built on Long Island as a surprise present for Zorina. He was also in the process of becoming an American citizen, something he remained proud of throughout his life. He was only sporadically involved with the School of American Ballet, which was flourishing under the eyes of Kirstein and Dimitriev, until finally Dimitriev was bought out— a relief to everyone, since he had grown more dictatorial and disagreeable than ever. (At one point he tried to throw Ruthanna Boris out of the school: "You go, go. Scholarship is finished. You go. You are Jew. Not for here. Jew. Go, go, go.") And Balanchine made no dances for Ballet Caravan, the small group founded and run by Kirstein, which concentrated on folklorish pieces of Americana, the most important of which was Eugene Loring's *Billy the Kid,* still performed effectively by many ballet companies.

By 1938 the American Ballet was all but dead. From the Stravinsky festival of 1937 until 1941 Balanchine created no new ballets of consequence, the longest such dry spell of his career. The problem was lack of opportunity, not lack of desire, although it was during this time that Lucia Chase founded Ballet Theatre (now American Ballet Theatre) and invited Balanchine to participate. Later he was to deny or forget that he had been offered this chance, but the offer is well documented. It isn't surprising that he turned his back on becoming part of a new organization: It was one thing to freelance occasionally, but if he was to involve himself seriously with a new company, it was going to be his own.

. . .

With the coming of the war and Europe under siege, the several Ballets Russes companies relocated to the United States and to endless touring. Balanchine's old nemesis Colonel de Basil hired him to stage several of his ballets for what was now called The Original Ballet Russe, and Balanchine gave them *Le Baiser de la Fée* and an expanded *Serenade*. One night, Balanchine, Stravinsky, and Tchelitchev went backstage to see Toumanova. "We want to give you a present—a diamond necklace," Balanchine said. The present was *Balustrade*, a new ballet to Stravinsky's Violin Concerto in D. Unfortunately, Zorina was to write, "Toumanova, who was so slim, had yards of tulle between her legs and large antlers on her head which hampered her movements. The beautiful choreography was practically invisible. I could have wept." *Balustrade* was performed only five times, but thirty years later, for the Stravinsky festival of 1972, Balanchine employed this same superb score for an entirely new ballet, *Stravinsky Violin Concerto*.

Another Balanchine-Stravinsky collaboration was somewhat more unlikely. Late in 1941 Balanchine was asked by the Ringling Brothers and Barnum & Bailey Circus to make a "ballet" for elephants. One of the hoary bits of Balanchine lore is that when he telephoned Stravinsky to invite him to write the music for a new ballet, Stravinsky asked, "For whom?" "For some elephants." "How old?" "Very young." "All right. If they are very young elephants, I will do it." The elephants were costumed in pale blue tutus, and the elephants were not amused. Although Marianne

Moore would write, "Their deliberate way of kneeling, on slowsliding forelegs—like a cat's yawning stretch or a ship's slide into water—is fine ballet," Vernon Duke remembered differently: "I can testify to the fact that the big beasts disliked their new music actively, refusing to dance to it and emitting ear-splitting roars." *The Ballet of the Elephants* (to Stravinsky's *Circus Polka*) lasted only one season. But earlier that year the opportunity for which Balanchine had been waiting had presented itself. Or, rather, Lincoln Kirstein had presented it to him.

When Kirstein's friend Nelson Rockefeller went to the State Department as Coordinator of Inter-American Affairs, the two men cooked up a novel plan: Kirstein and Balanchine would lead a group on an extended goodwill tour of Latin America in the summer of 1941. There would be a company of thirty-six dancers, pieced together from Ballet Caravan, the dormant American Ballet, and the school. Rockefeller came through with a government check "so large," Kirstein wrote, "that I was as scared as if I had stolen it." The company encountered all the usual mishaps, and a few novel ones as well. When they arrived in Buenos Aires, all the dancers under eighteen were arrested and taken to jail for the day on suspicion of having been imported for purposes of prostitution; Balanchine insisted on going with them. A blizzard high in the Andes immobilized the company for two weeks (Kirstein: "The Andes were impassable. Our scenery had to be routed, guarded by two dancers, up and through Bolivia"), delaying their opening in Santiago, Chile.

Dreary theaters, lost baggage, terrible food, all the standard problems of touring. But the tour was not a disaster. The company had five months of invaluable experience, giving more than a hundred performances; critics and audiences were tremendously enthusiastic; and—crucially—Balanchine had been given a chance to create two major ballets. Swiftly he choreographed both *Concerto Barocco* and *Ballet Imperial,* to Bach and Tchaikovsky, previewing both of them at an open rehearsal in New York late in May.

It was Nathan Milstein who had suggested Bach's D Minor Concerto for Two Violins to Balanchine, and he recalled Balanchine saying that he was attracted by two aspects of Bach: "the mathematical precision of his music and, at the same time, its purely emotional and unfeigned striving for God." Originally performed with decor and costumes by Eugene Berman, by the early fifties *Barocco* was being performed in the stripped-down version now seen around the world. Not only have its costumes changed; a certain jazziness to the steps has been ironed out, and *Barocco* now looks somewhat more solemn than it once did. (Fred Danieli, who was in the original cast, remembers that there was a movement in the adagio which Balanchine called the "Harlem strut." "There was a lot of kidding around in the rehearsals. We did that strut as a joke, and Balanchine liked it and kept it in.") But however *Barocco* is danced, its greatness has never been in doubt. For many it is Balanchine's signature work, and it is one of his most performed. Intricate yet calm, formal yet lively, abstract yet profoundly human, it pointed the way for-

ward, in much the same way that Fokine's *Les Sylphides* had done thirty-five years earlier, whereas *Ballet Imperial,* set to Tchaikovsky's Piano Concerto No. 2, looks backward to the classicism and grandeur of Petipa. (Some years later, when Ruthanna Boris asked Balanchine why he refused to revive Petipa's *Paquita,* he answered, "Because if we do *Paquita,* everybody will see what I stole for *Ballet Imperial.*") With its two daunting ballerina roles, its beautiful manipulations of the *corps,* and its echoes of *Swan Lake, Ballet Imperial* is both lyrical and explosive. Only the steely attack and strength of Marie-Jeanne—that all-American paragon of speed and clarity—made it and *Barocco* possible. (Balanchine's brief personal relationship with her was to be strained by her desire to have a normal marriage and children. Marie-Jeanne: "A child would have required something that he couldn't give." After she married, they continued to work together, but he never made another great role for her.)

It was clear by now that his relationship with Zorina was deteriorating. The marriage was obviously a failure. It had begun, she wrote, as if they were "two children playing a game. None of the weightier problems of marriage for us. No financial problems, no in-law problems, no household problems, no concern over babies. All serene and unclouded." It didn't stay that way. "George," Zorina went on, "put women on a pedestal, where they don't necessarily want to be. Women don't want to be idolized, which can be dehumanizing. It can be oppressive to be loved too much—even suffocating." They were often apart. She

had almost come on the South American tour, then didn't, and by 1943 was performing (with Balanchine's approval) at Ballet Theatre—in fact, one of her roles there was *Apollo*'s Terpsichore. But she had met the man she would eventually settle down with permanently, the distinguished classical-record producer Goddard Lieberson.

She and her mother moved into the Ritz Towers, and one night when Balanchine got back to New York, she greeted him with, "Your room is there at the end of the hall." It was the maid's room. According to Natalie Molostwoff, an adminstrator at the school and at that time a close friend of Balanchine's, "So he picked up his suitcase and left." During this time there was a fire at the school, and, Molostwoff says, "We rounded up the dancers. Balanchine and I stayed on until the last student left. He was cool, calm, and collected. 'I don't care,' he said. 'I just don't care now whether I live or not.'"

Many friends and colleagues testify to his despair. Taper says, "Sometimes he could be seen standing in the street outside her apartment for hours late at night, unshaven, haggard, thoroughly wretched, waiting for a glimpse of her." John Taras confirmed this to me, recalling how Balanchine would weep over his food at the ex-speakeasy Tony's. (Zorina's version: "Throughout the late spring and summer of 1945, George and I had gently drifted farther apart.") In January 1946 Zorina obtained a divorce in Reno; on April 2 she and Lieberson were married; on October 25 their first child was born.

·   ·   ·

With the war on and Kirstein away in the army, there was no chance for another company of his own. Balanchine had been occupying himself with a number of disparate projects: for Zorina, the "Old Black Magic" number in the all-star Paramount film *Star-Spangled Rhythm*; a few lackluster musicals and several that got away, including one with Vernon Duke to be based on a novel by Robert (*Portrait of Jennie*) Nathan, and a ballet-play for Zorina based on the life of the nineteenth-century ballerina Fanny Elssler—his collaborator, the future memoirist Alexander King; a series of very successful operettas, including *Rosalinda* (*Die Fledermaus*), *The Merry Widow,* and the romanticized version of the life of Grieg, *Song of Norway;* helping Zorina with her movement (as Ariel) in a Broadway production of *The Tempest*; his first original work for Ballet Theatre, *Waltz Academy*; a benefit performance of the *Saint Matthew Passion* (called *The Crucifixion of Christ*), conceived of and conducted by Leopold Stokowski, with Lillian Gish as Mary Magdalene; dances for several productions of the New Opera Company. But his main connection during this period was with Serge Denham's Ballet Russe de Monte Carlo.

It was through *Song of Norway* that he began his new association with the Ballet Russe. Denham had loaned his dancers, led by Danilova and Frederic Franklin, to the project, and Danilova proposed Balanchine as choreographer. The company was in poor shape, and Denham immediately understood how useful Balanchine could be, while Balanchine, although he didn't like Denham, nevertheless grasped the practical advantages of

having a classical company to work with. The two men agreed to agree, and Balanchine brushed up and cheered up the dispirited dancers, adding *Serenade, Concerto Barocco,* and *Ballet Imperial* to the repertory and beginning to make new ballets as well. For two years he worked and traveled with the Ballet Russe—a wonderful companion, according to Franklin, who sometimes roomed with him, and the dancer Todd Bolender, who reports hilarious dinners, with Balanchine telling endless bawdy jokes in his thick Russian accent.

Late in 1944 came *Danses Concertantes,* to a recent Stravinsky score, and a revival of Richard Strauss's *Le Bourgeois Gentilhomme,* which Balanchine had previously mounted on de Basil's company in 1932. And then, early in 1946, he created *Night Shadow* (later to be retitled *La Sonnambula*), to a Vittorio Rieti score based on themes by Bellini. This haunting work had two leading female roles, the Sleepwalker herself and the Coquette. Balanchine offered Danilova her choice, and she decided on the Sleepwalker, which was to become one of her most famous roles. The Coquette was performed by Maria Tallchief, a young dancer in whom Balanchine had become increasingly interested.

Tallchief had been born in 1925, the daughter of an Osage Indian father, Alexander Joseph Tall Chief, and a Scots-Irish mother. The family had money from the father's royalties from oil wells drilled on Osage land, and Mrs. Tall Chief had ambitions for her daughters (Maria's younger sister, Marjorie, was also to become an important dancer). When Tallchief was eight, the family moved from Oklahoma to Southern California, where

Marie (or Betty Marie, as she was then called; it was Agnes de Mille who pointed out to her that Betty was no name for a ballerina) continued her dance and piano lessons. She had perfect pitch and was an accomplished musician—when she was twelve, she gave a concert in which she played Bach and Mozart in the first half and danced in the second. But her ultimate devotion was to ballet, and she studied under the strict tutelage of Bronislava Nijinska, "the likes of [whom] were something I had never seen before." She worked with Nijinska for five years and, Tallchief has written, "Madame saw that I was serious."

By the time she was seventeen, in 1942, Tallchief had joined Denham's Ballet Russe as an apprentice, but soon she was doing solo roles and was promoted. She first encountered Balanchine professionally when he arrived on the Coast to choreograph *Song of Norway,* and when she returned from the operetta to the ballet company, he was soon singling her out. Her musicianship impressed him—she understood what he was doing. "He had the same steps and vocabulary of movement to work with as everyone else, but he broke down the inherent rhythm of the music to make the steps more exciting. It is this element of phrasing—the way the dynamics of a step relates to the tempo of the music—that makes the dance fit the score so beautifully. When I saw what he had done, I was astonished."

By studying the style and technique of dancers Balanchine favored—Mary Ellen Moylan, in particular—Tallchief began to understand what her own dancing lacked. And Balanchine made it clear to her that if she wanted to become a serious dancer, she

would have to go back to basics. "It meant that I virtually had to retrain myself, work harder than ever before. But I had seen the difference between Mary Ellen's dancing and mine. I knew he was right." As always, when a dancer trusted him and followed him completely, he gave everything back in return. And his interest in her grew more personal. One night, he asked her to meet him after a performance. "'Maria,' he said, 'I would like you to become my wife,' and he quickly added, 'Yes. I would like to marry you. I think it would be the most wonderful thing.' 'I . . . eh . . . ' I could barely speak, and the silence was awkward. I still called him Mr. Balanchine. Under the circumstances I thought it would be ludicrous. 'But, George,' I finally said. 'I'm not sure that I love you. I feel that I hardly know you.' 'That doesn't make any difference at all, Maria,' he said. 'We can get married and work together, and if it lasts, if it's only for a few years, that's fine. If it doesn't work, well, that's fine too.'" The next day when she mentioned to her friend Vida Brown that "George asked me to marry him," Brown responded, "George who?" When Tallchief explained, they both burst out laughing. But when Brown asked her, "Do you want to?" after a moment's thought she answered, "You know, I do." They were married in August 1946. Balanchine was forty-two, Tallchief was twenty-one.

There was another turning point in his life that year. Lincoln Kirstein was back from the army, and he and Balanchine came up with yet another approach to creating the kind of ballet company they both believed in. It was to be called Ballet Society, and

it was not to be sold directly to the general public but only by subscription to true believers, who would receive tickets for all performances and special events, a subscription to a scholarly publication called *Dance Index,* and various other perks. The press would not be invited; they would have to subscribe like everyone else (a typical Kirstein act of provocation). Their initial announcement succeeded in rounding up about eight hundred subscribers.

Balanchine dancers from the past—from the American Ballet, the Met, Denham's Ballet Russe, Ballet Caravan—were quick to attach themselves to Ballet Society: William Dollar, Gisella Caccialanza, Lew Christensen, Fred Danieli, Todd Bolender, John Taras, Elise Reiman, and Mary Ellen Moylan, among others, signed on. The opening performance took place on November 20, 1946, at the highly unlikely auditorium of New York City's Central High School of Needle Trades—a vast, uninviting space, whose stage was extremely shallow. The curtain came up late, but, wrote Anatole Chujoy in *Dance News,* "The long wait, the uncomfortable seats . . . were immediately forgotten, for there was magic on the stage."

There were two attractions. First came a new version of the Ravel-Colette *L'Enfant et les sortilèges (The Spellbound Child),* with roles doubled by singers and dancers. Of greater consequence was the other new ballet, *The Four Temperaments,* which would prove to be a landmark both for Balanchine and for ballet itself: This was the first of what are considered his ultramodern works, although it is firmly based on classical steps. It would not

fully reveal itself until 1951, when it was finally stripped of its impossibly ornate and obstructive Kurt Seligmann costumes; they had been progressively simplified through the intervening years. Back in 1940 Balanchine had some extra money from his Broadway earnings and decided that instead of buying himself something like a new cigarette case, he would personally commission a score from the German émigré composer Paul Hindemith, then teaching at Yale. Accounts differ as to whether he paid Hindemith $250 or $500. When the score was delivered, there was no company to set it on, but years later Ballet Society provided the opportunity. Balanchine was as patient as he was practical.

Despite its costumes, *The Four Temperaments* was quickly understood to be something new and important. Writing in the year of its premiere, Edwin Denby, then America's finest dance critic, summed it up: "No choreography was ever more serious, more vigorous, more wide in scope or penetrating in imagination. And none could be more consistently elegant in its bearing." *The Four Ts*, as it is affectionately called, is the precursor of *Agon* and *Episodes* and the other advanced black-and-white ballets—as radical a shift in ballet history as *Apollo* had been eighteen years earlier.

If the late thirties and the war period were characterized by a relative withdrawal from large-scale invention, the years 1946 through 1948 were one of those explosive creative moments that punctuated Balanchine's career—as if he had been storing up a series of masterpieces, only waiting for the occasion to release

them onto the stage. In July 1947, at the invitation of the Paris Opéra (from which Lifar was temporarily banned, owing to his ambiguous relations with the Germans during the occupation), he created—in two weeks!—the four-movement *Le Palais de cristal,* with Toumanova in the second-movement adagio, which has become perhaps the most coveted role in the Balanchine repertory. Under the name *Symphony in C,* this unprecedented outburst of classical dance invention, to an obscure symphony written by Bizet when he was seventeen, has provided countless audiences with pure pleasure. In Paris it was performed with elaborate decor by the surrealist artist Leonor Fini, each movement dressed in a different color. In America, when produced for Ballet Society a year later, and ever since, it has been in shimmering white and black.

Only four months later Balanchine made the elegant and demanding *Theme and Variations,* to Tchaikovsky, for Ballet Theatre, his only major work for that company. This piece, with its strong echoes of *The Sleeping Beauty,* is Balanchine's most direct tribute to strict Petipa classicism. The dancers' technique—or lack of it—is completely exposed. (Its ballerina role, originally performed by Alicia Alonso, and the Marie-Jeanne role in *Ballet Imperial* are perhaps the most difficult in the Balanchine repertory—the gut-crunchers, as they're sometimes called.) Igor Youskevitch, the original male lead, recalls that Balanchine kept trying to get him to be more abstract in the role: "He was always asking me to be less romantic." But *Theme* is as glittering and rousing as it is academic and formal. It's both a challenge and a

magnificent opportunity—one appreciated by generations of leading dancers.

For the final season of Ballet Society, in the spring of 1948, Balanchine created the last of this extraordinary run of masterpieces, *Orpheus,* with a commissioned score by Stravinsky and startling sculptural decor by Isamu Noguchi. By now, Tallchief was in the company, as was the future star Tanaquil LeClercq, who had grown up in the School of American Ballet. The year before, Balanchine had made what he thought of as a teaching ballet called *Symphonie Concertante,* featuring the two of them embodying the violin and viola parts of Mozart's charming score. At the time, LeClercq was a sixteen-year-old student. Now Tallchief would be Eurydice and LeClercq the Leader of the Bacchantes who tear Orpheus to pieces, while the leading male roles would be performed by two men who were to be mainstays of the male contingent for many years—Nicholas Magallanes and Francisco Moncion, as Orpheus and the Dark Angel.

The collaboration of Stravinsky and Balanchine on *Orpheus* was extremely close, with the composer attending rehearsals and conducting the premiere. (He was to say, "Never was I more personally involved than with this piece, which is the story of the artist.") After the plotless Balanchine ballets that had preceded it, a dance-drama like *Orpheus* came as a surprise to critics and the audience. "The choreography for Magallanes," John Taras has said, "was unlike anything Balanchine had done before. There were very few steps and no conventional ones. The movement was more like the miming of a song than the execution of a dance." For many years, *Orpheus* remained a central work in the

Balanchine repertory. Only with the move in 1964 from the relatively intimate City Center, with its small stage, to the much larger New York State Theater at Lincoln Center, together with the diminishing ability of young dancers to perform dramatic roles, did it recede in importance. To those like myself who first saw it in the year it was made, it was a formative dance experience.

The subscription season at the City Center in the spring of 1948 was followed by several performances open to the general public, a daring move on the part of Ballet Society. But the company had not only *Orpheus* but *Symphony in C* and several other new works to show New York. The critical reception was enthusiastic, even from John Martin. More important, Morton Baum, the financial director of the City Center—a peculiar building once known as the Mecca Temple—which the city had taken over in lieu of unpaid taxes, was deeply impressed. "I am in the presence of greatness," he told an associate, and immediately asked to see Lincoln Kirstein. At their meeting, Baum recalled, "Kirstein was belligerent, almost hostile to me, vituperative against the entire ballet field, its policies, managers, repertoire. He seemed not to believe in the sincerity of my call and was suspicious of everything I said." But when Baum suggested that Ballet Society should rename itself the New York City Ballet and make the City Center its permanent home, Kirstein exclaimed, "If you do that for us, I will give you in three years the finest ballet company in America."

What this meant for Balanchine was that twenty-four years after having left Russia, and fifteen years after arriving in America, he would at last have a permanent home and the continuity he had always lacked.

BALLERINAS

Above: With Tanaquil LeClercq

Below: Choreographing *The Seven Deadly Sins* with Allegra Kent

Opposite: With Maria Tallchief

With the anguish of his failed marriage to Zorina behind him and the promise of stability at the City Center, Balanchine was in a position to consolidate both his inner and outer lives. The relationship with Tallchief was gratifying professionally and easy emotionally. From the account in her autobiography, it's clear that although they were happy together, this was no grand passion (for either of them). "Work took precedence over everything. . . . Passion and romance didn't play a big role in our married life. We saved our emotion for the classroom." Dryly she informs us that "he made sure we slept in twin beds, perhaps to conserve his energy." He was always calm, affectionate, reasonable; interested in her clothes, her perfume (he chose L'Heure Bleue for her—she still uses it). He sent her charming little notes, most of them beginning, "Hi Darling!" And, she tells us, their relationship fulfilled her—until it didn't. (He once told the dancer Robert Weiss, "You know I loved Maria, great dancer, great woman, was like tiger. Being married

Opposite top: Choreographing *Agon.* On bench, center: Balanchine, Stravinsky, Lucia Davidova. Front: Diana Adams and Arthur Mitchell

Opposite bottom: Rehearsing *Movements for Piano and Orchestra* with Suzanne Farrell and Jacques d'Amboise

to tiger very exciting, but after awhile, being married to tiger takes too much energy.")

Professionally their relationship could hardly have been more fulfilling. New York City Ballet was in reality Ballet Society under a new name, and the core of the company remained the same. Tallchief dominated *Orpheus* and triumphed in the difficult first movement of *Symphony in C* when Balanchine restaged it in America. It perfectly suited her strong and assertive technique, her absolute command of the stage, and no one has ever improved on her performance in this role. (She was in Paris with Balanchine when he staged *Le Palais de cristal* at the Opéra, and he must have had her in mind as he created this part.) She had remade herself as a Balanchine dancer, and despite the presence of other talented women in the company, she remained, for half a dozen years, *the* Balanchine dancer.

Certainly she was perceived as the company's star—an impression confirmed in November 1949, when she was the key to its first bona fide hit, Balanchine's reworking of the Stravinsky-Fokine *Firebird,* with which Diaghilev had electrified Paris in 1910. Over dinner at the Russian Tea Room one night, the impresario Sol Hurok suggested that Balanchine restore *Firebird* "for your wife." Hurok was also ready and willing to sell to the New York City Ballet—for $4,250—the enchanting 1945 Chagall sets that he happened to be holding in storage. Balanchine speeded up the action, created new material, and, most important, unleashed Tallchief in an electric star performance that secured the company's future and certified City Ballet as a major force in the dance world.

Francisco Moncion, who danced the Prince, was to say, "The ballet was made for Maria, and she went after it like a demon, with ferocity, as if possessed." She herself recalled the crucial moment on opening night on which the ballet's success seemed to hang:

> In spite of all my practice, the variation was very difficult, and I was completely out of breath. But when we started the pas de deux, I felt secure. Standing upstage, I took an extra breath and then made the flying leap into Frank's arms. Suddenly there I was being held by him upside down, my head practically touching the floor. An audible sigh rose in the audience. . . . It was as if they could barely believe what they had seen. The second before I had been at one end of the stage standing upright, yet now here I was at the other side, suspended in Frank's arms. No one could see how it had been done. I must have flown. . . . The way [George] had been able to create that moment was astonishing even to me. I'd become this magical creature, the Firebird, yet I knew I had become the Firebird because George had made me the Firebird. His genius had never been as clear to me as it was in that instant.

Balanchine was to create role after role on Tallchief in these years: in *Bourrée Fantasque* (which premiered only four days after *Firebird*); in the *Sylvia Pas de Deux*, in *A la Françaix, Scotch Symphony, Pas de Dix* (from *Raymonda*), *Allegro Brillante,* and finally *Gounod Symphony*. She was the Siren in the 1950 revival of *Prodigal Son,* and the Terpsichore in the 1951 revival of *Apollo*.

Also in 1951 she provided another turning point in the company's coming-of-age, when she performed Odette in Balanchine's new one-act version of *Swan Lake,* also a smash hit. And perhaps most important, she was the Sugar Plum Fairy when in 1954 he created his first full-evening ballet, *The Nutcracker,* which cemented the company's financial stability (as it still does today). In the beginning, Tallchief danced all performances—there was no one else. She was the rock on which he built the New York City Ballet.

In these first few years a parade of accomplished dancers was joining and strengthening the company's core of Ballet Society veterans, most of the new hands coming from Ballet Theatre: Jerome Robbins, Melissa Hayden, Diana Adams, Nora Kaye, Hugh Laing, and Janet Reed (via Robbins's Broadway musical *Look, Ma, I'm Dancin'!*). The virtuoso classicist André Eglevsky had been the *premier danseur* of the Marquis de Cuevas's Grand Ballet. But the most compelling presence apart from Tallchief was, from the beginning, Tanaquil LeClercq, who unlike any of the others was a pure product of the School of American Ballet. She stood out even as a child, and by the age of sixteen she was a clear winner—tall, thin, elegant, witty, with a big jump and a sardonic grin. Tallchief was a powerhouse; LeClercq was a greyhound. When you watch clips of her today, you see a nonpareil: irreplaceable for her jazzy grace. Her jauntiness in the final movement of *Western Symphony,* her wicked glee in *Bourrée Fantasque* (hilariously paired with Jerry Robbins), the *snap* of her *Concerto Barocco* have never been equaled. But she was also perhaps the

greatest of those who have danced the adagio second movement of *Symphony in C*—only Allegra Kent and Suzanne Farrell can be thought of as her equals. And then, in 1951, Balanchine defined her forever when he created *La Valse,* to Ravel.

This ballet, filled with foreboding, with its ravishing Karinska "New Look" ball gowns and heavily atmospheric lighting, was an immediate success, and it changed the way we looked at LeClercq. Until then she had been a radiant colt; now she was a doomed young woman, whose attraction to Death (Moncion) at the height of the ball's frenzy, made her disturbingly complicit in her fate—a far more complicated creature than we had previously understood her to be. *La Valse* looks back to the overheated dramatic romanticism of *Cotillon.* Alas, the tragic fate of the heroine also anticipates the personal fate of LeClercq.

Balanchine's marriage to Tallchief—a marriage of mutual admiration and shared achievement—was not so much unraveling as slipping away, as she put it. She was strong-minded, and she wanted a more stimulating life offstage than Balanchine was interested in or capable of providing. She wanted, among other things, a domestic as well as a professional partner—a lover, and children. In 1952 their marriage was annulled. By then she had found another man, and Balanchine had focused on LeClercq.

According to Bernard Taper, "The first words Tanaquil LeClercq remembers hearing from her future husband, George Balanchine, were a reprimand. He told her that she was a naughty, saucy child, who was putting on gestures so mannered and affectedly pretty that he could not bear to look at her. Then he

sent her out of the room. That was when she was twelve. . . . For her part, on first impression, she thought the famous Mr. Balanchine something of an old fogy and a very dull teacher, and she could not see what was supposed to be so great about him." They both quickly changed their minds, and by the time she was in her mid-teens, she was being propelled toward stardom. She was from the start—like Allegra Kent, Patricia McBride, and Darci Kistler later on—one of those dancers whom audiences took to their hearts as well as admired. In her brief career she was to inhabit such diverse works as the buggy *Metamorphosis,* the exquisite *Divertimento No. 15,* the Dew Drop sequence of *Nutcracker* (another role in which she has never been surpassed), as well as Frederick Ashton's *Illuminations* (she was Sacred Love) and Robbins's *Afternoon of a Faun* and *The Concert.* She and Robbins were to remain lifelong friends.

When LeClercq and Balanchine married, on December 31, 1952, she was twenty-three and he was forty-eight. Kirstein wrote to Richard Buckle, "At midnight we all foregathered. As the Russians and Russians continued to troop in, Tanny said to me: 'Oh, my God, what Have I Let Myself IN FOR?'" Nothing changed professionally between Balanchine and Tallchief—he went on creating major roles for her, and as with his other ex-wives, he remained on happy terms with her for the rest of his life—but LeClercq was clearly the ballerina of the future.

Then in the fall of 1956, in Copenhagen—the company was on tour—she was suddenly taken ill. The frightening rumor was

that it was meningitis. In an as-yet-unpublished memoir, Barbara Milberg, then a company soloist, quotes Vida Brown, then the ballet mistress, who at the time was sharing a room with Melissa Hayden in the hotel where the Balanchine party was staying:

> One night, at about 5:30 A.M., there was a knock on our door, and when I opened it, Balanchine was there, standing in the hall. He looked drawn, pale, somehow shrunken. "Come in, come in." No, he just stands there speechless in the doorway. "What is it? What's the matter?" And Balanchine is finally able to say the words. "It's Tanny. She has polio." I put my arms around him and started to cry. We both started to cry. Then Millie put her arms around us, and all three of us were weeping. I didn't know what to do or say, so I asked if he wanted me to order coffee. He just retreated back into the hallway and leaned against the wall.

Barbara Horgan, then the company's assistant manager, remembers that on that morning of November 1, the day they were scheduled to travel on to Stockholm, her phone rang very early, and she was asked to come at once to Betty Cage's room. When she got there, Betty—the company's formidable manager—was in tears and told her that Tanny had been diagnosed with polio and was not expected to live. How to tell the company? And how to keep going? The decision was made to continue the tour, though of course Balanchine stayed on in Copenhagen.

Tanny's mother, Edith LeClercq, was there, helping to care for her, and in his odd hours, to distract himself, Balanchine staged

several of his ballets for the Royal Danes. Otherwise, he would sit with Tanny for hours, reading to her, encouraging her. In his hotel room he cooked and played solitaire. To Betty Cage, back in New York, he wrote, "Tanny is getting along slowly. God will help us, I believe. . . ." To Kirstein he wrote, "Edith and I are trying to be cheerful. We are hoping and hoping and hoping and waiting." His grief was compounded by an irrational or superstitious guilt he felt because when Tanny had been a girl of fifteen, he had featured her in a March of Dimes benefit at the Waldorf-Astoria, in which a grim figure in black came forward and struck her down with polio. In the ballet she was miraculously restored. To Taper, Balanchine said, "It was, alas, a balletic finale. Nothing like that ending will happen in Tanny's real life."

Not until March of the following year was LeClercq strong enough to be flown to New York and to Lenox Hill Hospital, where she stayed for some time before going for treatment to Warm Springs, Georgia, the spa that President Roosevelt, the world's most famous polio victim, had made celebrated. Presumably, although the doctors had made it clear that the paralysis of her legs was permanent, the Balanchines continued to hope. When they returned to New York, for months Balanchine stayed home with his wife. "George did everything possible for her—and more," wrote Nathan Milstein, who visited them frequently during this period. "He was husband, father, physician, nursemaid. He cooked for her, he invented special exercises." The irony was that before LeClercq was struck down by the disease, she and Balanchine had more or less agreed to go their separate (domestic) ways. Now he committed himself to her totally.

Throughout the first year of LeClercq's illness, he stayed away from the company, which seemed rudderless and depressed, deprived both of its leader and of its most dazzling dancer. In May 1956, before the fateful European tour, Balanchine had created one of his most beautiful works, *Divertimento No. 15*. It was to be a year and a half before he returned to the studio and choreography. But when he did, it was with the characteristic burst of creative energy that he always displayed after a dry spell. Late in 1957, in less then two months, he created four major works, and they were of an astonishing variety and quality. *Gounod Symphony* was a subtle period piece reflecting the tone of nineteenth-century Paris Opéra ballets—a kind of gentler companion to the equally French *Symphony in C*. It was made for Tallchief, but its qualities found a more congenial proponent when the French Violette Verdy joined the company a year or so later. Despite its felicities, *Gounod* has had only a half-life (or quarter-life) in the repertory, emerging only sporadically, although it remained a favorite of Kirstein's.

Square Dance was a lively, almost rambunctious mix of the baroque music of Vivaldi and Corelli and American square dancing, caller and all—"Two little ladies, up the track, Sashay over, sashay back . . ." Sparked by the dynamic Patricia Wilde, it was an instant favorite, and almost twenty years later, in a new version, it became a company staple. I remember Balanchine explaining at a board of directors meeting in the seventies: "We need new ballet. No money. I take *Square Dance*, get rid of caller—too expensive. We already have music parts. Put in practice costumes.

Add one new solo for Bart Cook—and we have new ballet!"

Stars and Stripes was a slam-bang crowd-pleaser, to a score adapted by Hershy Kay from John Philip Sousa. Some people were offended by what appeared to be the ballet's blatant patriotism—it ends with a giant American flag scrolling up against the back of the stage while the entire company, forty-odd strong, stands and salutes. But of course it was much more. It was a brilliant classical ballet masquerading as a popular entertainment, with a final *pas de deux* (for Melissa Hayden and Jacques d'Amboise) whose parodic tone camouflaged its severe academic demands. Just before the premiere the critic Walter Terry ran into Balanchine and asked him if the new ballet had a story. "Yes," Balanchine said. "The United States."

The great event of the season, though—and one of the peaks of Balanchine's entire career—was the premiere of *Agon*, on December 1, 1957. This ballet was the culmination of what had by then become a thirty-year collaboration between Balanchine and Stravinsky. His admiration for the composer was boundless; his veneration of the older man was that of a son for a father. Tallchief was to comment, in *I Remember Balanchine*, "When I was married to Balanchine, I must say there were times when his love of Stravinsky, his adulation for the man, seemed too much. He idolized him. As always, George was right."

Unlike some revolutionary works, *Agon* was appreciated from the start. At once it was clear to everyone that Balanchine had carried ballet forward into uncharted territory. Its spiky, difficult music and restrained but innovative steps; the contrast of its ex-

treme modernity with its echoes of ancient court dances—the gailliard, the sarabande; the shock (remember, this was 1957) of the central *pas de deux* in which Balanchine paired the glamorous, pale Diana Adams with Arthur Mitchell, the handsome young black dancer who was to go on to found the Dance Theatre of Harlem—all these things riveted critics and audiences from the very first. Edwin Denby wrote of the enormous impact of the opening night: "The balcony stood up shouting and whistling when the choreographer took his bow. Downstairs, people came out into the lobby, their eyes bright as if the piece had been champagne. Marcel Duchamp, the painter, said he felt the way he had after the opening of Le Sacre." But the premiere of the Stravinsky-Nijinsky *Sacre du printemps* had been a scandal; the premiere of *Agon* was an overwhelming triumph. It was *Agon* that brought home to the dance world that Balanchine was indeed a supreme master; that he could do anything. It seemed to cap his already amazing fecundity—except that there were twenty-five years of choreography to come.

Agon's ballerina, Diana Adams, was a complicated figure. Offstage she was anxious, insecure; onstage, coolly perfect—an icy and frightening Siren in *Prodigal Son,* for instance. ("One look from her menacing, steely eyes," wrote Edward Villella, "would send a shudder through my body.") Composed and calm, she was very different from her great friend Tanny LeClercq, who was so witty, so funny—who made Balanchine laugh when she would do silly things like bark like a dog. When Balanchine

became passionate about Diana, it must have been impossibly difficult and painful. "He was really in love with her," Lucia Davidova reported, "but his wife was an invalid and he didn't know what to do about it. He tried for three years or so. Then finally he said to his wife, as he told me, 'Tanny, if I go on with this marriage, I think I'll stop creating. . . . In order to continue working I have to follow my love.'" Adams had become an obsessive focus, but she was unobtainable; apart from everything else, she was determined to have children, and having married Ronnie Bates, the company's stage manager, she eventually, and happily, gave birth to a daughter. "When Diana left him he was disconsolate," Davidova testified. "He said, 'Somebody just put their hand on my head and is holding me under water, and I don't know when I'll come up.'" "When he was taking care of Tanny during that period," wrote the dancer and ballet mistress Janet Reed, "he was having fainting spells. They were panic attacks. I didn't know anything about them in those days. I do now, having had a few myself. I know what he went through."

During the fifties, when Balanchine was drawing away from LeClercq, a very young new dancer, Allegra Kent, caught his attention. He could hardly have missed her—from her first appearances on stage, when she was fifteen and sixteen, she stood out with her exquisite beauty and her supremely natural talent. Not only could she do anything, but she seemed to do it all with no apparent difficulty or strain. When she was seventeen, in 1954, he created his first role for her, in "The Unanswered Question" section of *Ivesiana,* a dark and mysterious work. Borne aloft

by four men, the barefoot girl, her hair down, dressed in a simple white leotard, is never allowed to touch the ground, while the man who yearns for her, earthbound, cannot capture her. Is she a dream? A vision? A memory? Allegra Kent remained an enigma, adored by audiences and Balanchine alike, still remembered as unique in the roles that became identified with her: the Sleepwalker in the revival of *La Sonnambula* he mounted for her; the dancing Anna in the revival of *The Seven Deadly Sins* (after twenty-five years, Lotte Lenya was back as the singing Anna); in the "Concerto" section of *Episodes*; as the delicate-erotic bride in *Bugaku*. (LeClercq called her "a rubber orchid.")

Kent was the Prodigal Daughter—in and out of the company for thirty years, welcomed back after having her babies (three of them); sometimes erratic, always unique. There was no question of a sexual relationship between her and Balanchine. Again and again he presented her as sensual yet also innocent, untouchable, virginal (until the stylized consummation of *Bugaku*). He was obviously fond of her, deeply excited by her talent, and slightly nervous of her—she was elusive, fey, unpredictable. He said she was a Brigitte Bardot (high praise!). But wonderful as she was—in *Apollo, Serenade, Symphony in C*—she didn't and wouldn't belong to him unreservedly.

It was natural, therefore, that eventually he would turn to a young dancer who, more than any other, *did* commit herself to him without reservation. She arrived at the school in 1960—no doubt the deeply religious Balanchine believed she had been sent

by God as his perfect instrument—and her art, her person, and her career were to transform and convulse New York City Ballet. She came from Cincinnati, and her name was Roberta Sue Ficker, soon to be changed to Suzanne Farrell. Diana Adams, touring the country in a talent search funded by the Ford Foundation, had discovered her and suggested that she audition for Mr. B. Awarded a full scholarship at the school, she was soon in the company and very quickly the object of Balanchine's interest. She was beautiful, talented, with a deep musicality and a powerful dance intelligence. From the start it was clear that she would try anything, do anything, *be* anything that he required. "If he thought I could do something, I would believe him," she wrote in her autobiography, *Holding On to the Air*, "often against my own reasoning. I trusted him not to let me be a fool, but rather a tool, an instrument in his hands. In short, I trusted him with my life." Here, finally, was the dancer whose commitment was as passionate and total as his own. Violette Verdy, the most analytical of Balanchine's ballerinas, has said, "I think that the person who has come closest to surrendering to Balanchine is Suzanne Farrell. She has managed that kind of wonderful surrender that is also a glorification of the self."

Everything conspired to advance her progress. In 1963 a new ballet—*Movements for Piano and Orchestra*—was being rehearsed by Diana Adams and Jacques d'Amboise to a new score by Stravinsky. This was when Adams became pregnant, and she had to withdraw. At d'Amboise's urging, the role was entrusted to Farrell, not yet eighteen and still in the *corps de ballet*. Adams

and d'Amboise taught it to her in Adams's living room—with no music—and within days Farrell was demonstrating it to Balanchine and Stravinsky at a rehearsal for which she was late because of an algebra exam at school.

Farrell triumphed in *Movements,* and soon afterward, Balanchine made his first ballet specifically for her—*Meditation,* a highly emotional duet in which an older man (d'Amboise again) conjures up in memory a young woman he has loved. So explicit a statement of love for such a newcomer could not go unnoticed, and soon what everyone suspected was confirmed: Balanchine was in thrall to Farrell. If further proof was needed, it came two years later with his three-act ballet *Don Quixote.* The old, befuddled, yet noble Don is inspired, cared for, tantalized by his servant, Dulcinea—a symbol of both purity and sensuality. At the first performance Balanchine himself played Don Quixote, and it was obvious that he was dancing not only *with* Farrell but *for* her. This was both a coronation (he called her an "alabaster princess") and a declaration of personal worship.

Offstage the intensity of his feelings was made equally clear. Company class was dominated by whatever aspect of her technique he thought needed working on. He stood in the wings every night watching her, and when the curtain came down on whatever ballet she was in, he would leave the theater with her, ignoring the dances and dancers that followed. Naturally there was resentment of her special position, both from established ballerinas and from other young girls hoping to draw Mr. B's attention. A combination of Balanchine's possessiveness and obses-

siveness and Farrell's natural reserve isolated her from the company. Several senior dancers left, making their reasons explicit: When Patricia Neary quit, Balanchine said to her, "I have the right to love." "You should love all eighty of us," was her reply. Maria Tallchief, for a dozen years the unproclaimed prima ballerina of City Ballet, famously remarked, "I don't mind being listed alphabetically, but I do mind being *treated* alphabetically." Balanchine was unmoved. Not only was Farrell his alabaster princess, she was his "pussy-cat fish"—though not just any cat or fish, Farrell herself has explained. The cat was a cheetah, for speed; the fish was a dolphin, for intelligence. After a performance of *Don Quixote* one night, he told Richard Buckle, "I have seen every dancer, and there has never been one like her. She can do everything."

Their personal relationship intensified. They were together constantly, with the approval of Farrell's mother, who, unlike Madame Toumanova, had encouraged the relationship from the start. But Balanchine's passion for Farrell and her feelings for him were apparently not consummated. He was still married to LeClercq, and Farrell was a devout Catholic. And he also was forty-one years older than she—despite his vigor and charm, an alarmingly older man. Possibly she felt that she was not only an alabaster princess but a captive one. For whatever combination of reasons, his longing for her grew, and her resistance persisted. Tallchief remembers Farrell saying, "Well, I'm the one who got away."

Of all the relationships with women he idealized but could not, finally, possess, this was perhaps the most tragic, since he

must have felt that he was being rejected as an old man. He was to tell Solomon Volkov: "It's hard to talk to young women when you're not so young, when you're over fifty. If they're seventeen, they want seventeen-year-old friends. Of course, you can be philosophical about it: what is, is, what will be, will be. But it can still annoy you, especially if you don't want simply to make a nice impression but are seriously attracted. . . . If you're interested in one of them a lot, that can hurt deeply. Love is a very important thing in a man's life, especially toward the end. More important than art."

Farrell rationalized the situation this way: "Balanchine needed to choreograph to live, just as I needed to dance to live. Neither of us needed to be married to live." Even so, he moved out of the apartment he shared with LeClercq and eventually obtained a Mexican divorce from her in order to be free to marry Farrell. She, however, fell in love with a young dancer in the company, Paul Mejia (who had been something of a favorite of Balanchine's), and married him—when Balanchine was out of the country. Barbara Horgan was summoned to join him and vividly recalls how distraught he was. When he returned, the situation became intolerable. Balanchine took roles away from Mejia, and Farrell stood by her husband. One night—the night of the premiere of Jerome Robbins's *Dances at a Gathering*—Farrell was meant to be dancing *Symphony in C.* Mejia was not cast in a role he felt he had a right to, and Farrell sent Balanchine an ultimatum: If Paul didn't dance that night, they would both resign. Balanchine ignored her warning, removed her, too,

from the performance, and Farrell was gone from the company. On every level this was traumatic—for her, for Balanchine, and for New York City Ballet as a whole, which for the previous half dozen years had been dominated by her presence.

That was in 1969, and the next few years were to be marked by personal and artistic retrenchment. The ballerina ranks were thin—older dancers were either gone or no longer at their peak, younger ones not fully developed. To a great extent, the company was sustained during this period by a dancer completely opposite to Farrell in look and temperament, the lyrical and ebullient Patricia McBride, not mysterious and grand but the epitome of the normal, all-American girl. She was small, very pretty, energetic, and alluring, and as useful to Robbins as to Balanchine. The first major work Balanchine made after Farrell's departure was *Who Cares?* to Gershwin songs, and it featured McBride triumphantly. Her happy and apparently uncomplicated nature, revealed in her clear yet expressive dancing, was the perfect antidote for a traumatized company and a disoriented audience.

The other superbly gifted dancer who emerged during this difficult time was Gelsey Kirkland, whose youth and apparent delicacy belied her perfect technique and troubled nature. Soon, however, she was gone, to dance with Baryshnikov and American Ballet Theatre and eventually to allow her career to self-destruct. (In her notorious autobiography, *Dancing on My Grave*, she blames Balanchine for much of what befell her—the only ballerina I can think of who has expressed anything other than awe and love for him.) To strengthen the ranks he chose two young

dancers to develop, Kay Mazzo and Karin von Aroldingen, both of whom were to serve him honorably and faithfully for many years.

While Balanchine recovered himself and moved forward with the 1972 Stravinsky festival, Farrell remained in exile, mostly working with the Maurice Béjart company in Brussels. She wasn't, however, doing what she was born to do, and no one knew that better than she did—unless it was Balanchine. In the summer of 1974 she wrote to him: "Dear George, As wonderful as it is to see your ballets, it is even more wonderful to dance them. Is this impossible? Love, Suzi." In January 1975 she—though not her husband, Paul—was back where she belonged. The personal relationship was never again what it had been, but the artistic partnership resumed, and once again Balanchine was deploying her genius to help fulfill his own. Farrell's return to City Ballet changed everything, just as her original domination of it had, and her departure had as well. She quickly recaptured her earlier repertory, dancing with greater depth and beauty than ever before, and Balanchine began making new roles on her—she was, after all, only twenty-eight at the time of her return. The ultimate word on the Farrell story was spoken by Delia Peters, one of the company's wits: "Suzanne's coming back is the best thing that's happened to us since she left."

If Farrell was the last of Balanchine's great muses (and passions), the first was probably Toumanova, "the black pearl" of the ballet, with whom he was or wasn't in love in the early thirties. There

are different versions of their story—if there *was* a story. When Kirstein was in Paris in 1933 in search of a choreographer, he reported in his journal that Bébé Berard had told him, "Balanchine is in love with Tamara Toumanova, whose mother says he is old enough to be her father (at twenty-nine?)." If she was born in 1919, as she claimed, she would have been fourteen at the time—about the age Geva was when he fell in love with her. Natalie Molostwoff says, "Tamara Toumanova left him, definitely. I think she was in love with someone," but that could have been later. Certainly, Mama Toumanova discouraged any talk of marriage: In the early thirties George was not that great a catch for her Tamara. Tallchief is certain that there was no romance between them, and Toumanova spoke of him as if he were an older brother, or even a father: "How he took care of me: he used to tell Mama what to do, what food to give me, not to overdo! . . . I really think that Balanchine looked upon me as his own child. He would play with me." He also loved Mama and Papa "because he found a family." She also thinks he felt a kinship with her "with my *tristesse,* with my being part Georgian. Because his sister, Tamara, died, I have a feeling that he looked upon me as a sister." Indeed, when she married, Balanchine turned up uninvited at the wedding in California. "Georgi Melitonovich, how incredible. You are here." And, she tells us, he replied, "How can I miss the marriage of my daughter?"

Brother, father, rejected suitor—who knows? What's certain is that he was fascinated by her looks and her dancing (as was most of the ballet world), that she inspired *Cotillon, Concurrence,*

Balustrade, and *Symphony in C,* and that they stayed close throughout their lives. In the forties, with Toumanova already something of a film star, they almost made a movie together about Anna Pavlova. Igor Youskevitch reported, "We all met in Hollywood. The movie was never made, but we rehearsed for a good six weeks, having a very good time. . . . We did not rehearse enough to have an idea of what the choreography would have been. Balanchine hung a rope in the studio, and Tamara did some pirouettes around it. Balanchine was trying different ideas." We can only regret that this outlandish project fell through.*

It seems appropriate to narrate Balanchine's life in relation to the women he was focused on, but there is another story, which is his relationship with his male dancers—a complicated dynamic of control, competition, and resentment combined with extraordinary creativity. A number of his important male dancers had difficulties with him, or he with them. His resentment of Serge Lifar lasted throughout his life—not because of the way Lifar betrayed him after Diaghilev's death, but because he was forced to comply with Diaghilev's determination to make Lifar a star. When William Weslow, a clever, charming, gossipy dancer in City Ballet, who felt relatively at ease with Balanchine, once asked him who his favorite male dancer was, Balanchine replied, "I've never liked the male dancer. Maybe one. Lifar—beautiful, almost

---

*In 1953, in the movie *Tonight We Sing,* a ludicrous version of the life of Sol Hurok, Toumanova finally gets to be Pavlova, performing Fokine's *The Dying Swan.*

like woman. And so I liked him because he was like woman. He was pretty, very girly, you know, beautiful legs and feet and poses. Like I do with girls, I used to pose him." So much for Serge Lifar.

Weslow also makes much of the mutual distrust and dislike between Balanchine and the great Danish dancer Erik Bruhn, who twice joined the company (and who was a close friend of Tallchief's, as well as the lover of Rudolf Nureyev). "Erik was a great star when he came," Weslow reports. "Balanchine hated his soul. . . . He did things to Erik like quickening the tempo. . . . 'No, no, too slow. Must be fast. You may be star in Denmark, dear, but this is my company. We must all dance fast here, and we don't want applause here to ruin sound of music.'" And he told his conductor, Robert Irving, "I don't like this Danish dancer here being a big star; everyone's a star in my company. He's nothing special." Bruhn, Weslow says, was in tears, and soon he left the company.

Perhaps the experience with Bruhn was in his mind when he told Nureyev, who hoped to join City Ballet, to go away and come back later, when he was tired of dancing his princes. When, years after this, Mikhail Baryshnikov *did* join the company—and Baryshnikov was then unquestionably the greatest and most successful dancer in the world—Balanchine made it clear that he wasn't going to get star treatment.

Baryshnikov was thrown into a wide assortment of roles with very little preparation, a problem compounded by the fact that he hadn't been trained in Balanchine technique and wasn't young

enough to absorb a new way of dancing overnight. He had joined the company with the highest expectations, but the physical difficulties he encountered combined with the fact that Balanchine, already unwell, couldn't create ballets on him, led to his leaving after a year and a half when he was offered the opportunity to run ABT. Billy Weslow, with his streak of witty malice, suggests that Balanchine deliberately kept Baryshnikov from exploiting his great capacities: "You don't have to do the bravura stuff. Just do something low, something simple." But among the many Balanchine roles to which Baryshnikov brought his luster were the Edward Villella specialities, and no one could call them low or simple. The experiment had been well worth making—invigorating City Ballet, stimulating Baryshnikov. And the two men got along well personally, comfortably reminiscing (in Russian, of course) about their early experiences in St. Petersburg. They remained friends after Baryshnikov's departure, and Baryshnikov at once expanded ABT's Balanchine repertory.

Bruhn and Baryshnikov were temporary phenomena, quickly moving on elsewhere with their brilliant careers. The most complicated of Balanchine's extended relationships with a male dancer was with Villella, a tough Italian-American kid from Bayside, Queens, who both worshipped Balanchine and fought him. Villella had attended the School of American Ballet as a boy (where he caught the attention of Jerry Robbins, who was inspired by him to create *Afternoon of a Faun*), but then had quit for the Merchant Marine Academy because his father was de-

termined that he get a college degree. As soon as he came back, having missed four crucial years of preparing to be a dancer, Balanchine was featuring him—his speed, his jump, his dazzling star power were irresistible. Balanchine went on to make a series of remarkable roles on him, from the "Rubies" section of *Jewels* to Harlequin in *Harlequinade* to the dazzling *Tarantella* to the fiendishly challenging Oberon in *A Midsummer Night's Dream*. Most tellingly, in 1960, he revived *Prodigal Son* for Villella, the role that became most closely associated with him. He was perfect for it—not just in look but in attitude and ability; but there was undoubtedly a message being sent with this piece of casting: "Defy me and see what happens—you'll have to crawl back." One of the ways Villella resisted Balanchine was in not attending his company class; because of the physical problems resulting from the gap in his training, he felt he needed the kind of help he could get only from Stanley Williams, the superb British-born teacher from Denmark whom Balanchine had imported for the school. This was the kind of resistance Balanchine did not accept easily, but his disapproval was rarely expressed openly. "Balanchine abhorred anything that might create confrontation," Villella wrote, "and everyone took the cue from him. We just swallowed hard and put up with what he dished out. We had to carry around our feelings of pain and rejection—and anger. We couldn't express them to his face." Villella not only titled his auto-biography *Prodigal Son*, but eventually he returned to his ballet father—not crawling, but honoring: His Miami City Ballet is one of the most dedicated Balanchine companies in the world today.

There were men with whom Balanchine did get along easily. In the early days the male contingent of the company included Nicholas Magallanes and Francisco Moncion, both of whom were superb partners but neither of whom was a strictly classical dancer; they had to be presented carefully, as in *Orpheus*. Nicky Magallanes was a universal favorite, gentle, unassuming, and reliable, and during the LeClercq years, he was part of what some dancers in the company referred to as the Royal Family, along with Balanchine, Tanny, Tanny's mother, Edith, and Diana Adams—people who clearly felt comfortable with one another. Richard Buckle remembers that when City Ballet was in London, the Balanchines shared a house with Magallanes and another dancer, Roy Tobias. "One morning as I was arriving to keep an appointment with Balanchine, Roy told me, 'He's gone to the laundry with Nick.' I was astounded: '*George Balanchine* has taken the *laundry*!' Roy confessed later, 'It was the first time I saw Balanchine with different eyes. He had always been just one of the family, and now I realized that people outside might look on him as something sacred.'"

(It's always touching to catch flashes of the "normal" life Balanchine lived, and of the contrast between his Olympian genius and control and his unassuming daily demeanor. Barbara Milberg remembers how on a European tour, in Florence, Balanchine, the dancer Frank Hobi, and the conductor/pianist Simon Sadoff all bought Vespas and decided to try them out. "We were on the train heading back to Paris and for a while we could see the three of them on a road that paralleled the track—

but not for long. 'There they are! There they are!' They came by, they waved—very happy, very windblown—and they disappeared into the dark." Three guys having fun. And Pat Wilde talks about weekends she spent with Balanchine and Tanny in Connecticut in the mid-fifties: "My husband and Mr. B. would spend the weekend cooking and working around outside. They built a little toolhouse and had various projects, and I would be busy baking bread. He was very informal in the country, always going around with his shirt off, working, getting the sun, digging around at the roses, cutting the grass. We'd start cooking in the afternoon and then sunbathe. Tamara Geva and her husband would come over. . . . Mr. B loved to talk about science or the movies—anything but dancing.")

Moncion was stalwart and endlessly useful. As modest as Magallanes, he had attended the school, was a charter member of Ballet Society and City Ballet, and danced countless roles through the decades. "We dubbed Balanchine father," he wrote in *I Remember Balanchine,* "but I don't think it was returned that way; that would have entailed a tremendous amount of responsibility. He was concerned primarily with the company, with the dancing. He used people as they came and went, the ebb and flow." When it finally became clear to Moncion that he was no longer wanted, Balanchine couldn't tell him directly. "I felt he wanted to get rid of me, and I wasn't ready to go." (Well, very few dancers *are* ready to go—they always feel they're too young to retire.) "For forty years I'd lived with the man," Moncion concluded, "worked for him, revered him, suffered with him, hated

him, loved him. The man was a genius and he had clay feet. No one's perfect."

The male dancer who was the chief exception to the rule was Jacques d'Amboise, who joined the company when he was fifteen, quickly became a leading dancer and a star presence, and kept going well into the Peter Martins era. He started out with less than perfect technique but worked hard, and was soon central to City Ballet's repertory. He was a famous Apollo, and starting in 1954, Balanchine made a series of roles on him, from *Western Symphony*—matching the fun and flair of LeClercq—to *Stars and Stripes* (tearing the house down with the equally slam-bang Melissa Hayden). In 1963 he began his partnership with Suzanne Farrell—*Movements for Piano and Orchestra, Meditation,* then the revival of *Ballet Imperial,* and eventually the "Diamonds" section of *Jewels.* In 1970 Balanchine created what is possibly d'Amboise's most characteristic role, the man (partnering three girls—*Apollo* redux) in the Gershwin *Who Cares?,* which seemed to sum up his cocky, open, American expansiveness and good humor. As late as 1980, more than thirty years after his joining the company, he was cast in a major new Balanchine ballet, *Robert Schumann's "Davidsbündlertänze."* Through his career at City Ballet, d'Amboise was on good terms with Balanchine, whom he knew how to please offstage as well as on—he was helpful and charming, and unthreatening. There were those who wondered why it was Peter Martins, not d'Amboise, who eventually secured the succession.

As for Martins, he joined City Ballet by accident—in 1967,

the company was in Edinburgh, on tour, and d'Amboise was injured; Martins was flown in to replace him in *Apollo* opposite Farrell. ("Well, at least he's tall," she remarked.) He was extraordinarily handsome, a true *danseur noble,* and a magnificent partner, but for some time there was a quality of sleepwalking to his performances. Feeling neglected after Farrell's departure, when he was no longer needed as her partner, he decided to quit and join ABT, then at the last moment held back. When he confronted Balanchine, he was shocked to discover that Balanchine thought he didn't care. "When people show interest, I use them. If they don't, I leave them alone. And you don't show interest." In other words, as Balanchine so frequently put it, "Show me, dear."

When Martins began to show him, Balanchine responded by creating two great roles for him during the 1972 Stravinsky festival—*Stravinsky Violin Concerto* and *Duo Concertant*—and from then on, Martins was the reigning prince, showing real talent as a choreographer as well as a dancer. Before that could happen, though, Martins had had to go through the Prodigal Son ritual: resistance, submission. But he was intelligent enough to understand that this submission was not to the man Balanchine but to the artist: "One eye on him and I knew what dancing was all about." By the end, it was he who was Balanchine's choice to succeed to the company. Balanchine made that very clear to me as we were standing in the wings together one evening. "It has to be Peter," he said, watching Martins and Farrell, and, I'm sure, speaking less to me personally than to me as a member of the board of directors. "He knows what a ballerina

needs." He said it again on another occasion. And in a long "conversation" between Balanchine and W. McNeil "Mac" Lowry published in *The New Yorker* soon after Balanchine's death, he refers to Martins over and over in a way that makes it clear who he felt his successor had to be. But there was no direct announcement; Martins just slipped into running things during Balanchine's long final illness and, after the usual flurries of temperament and politics, was eventually ratified by the board as co-director with Robbins.

Balanchine had always said that it would all be over when he was gone, that you couldn't hold on to ballets, that everything would inevitably change. But there was going to be a future whether he liked it or not—City Ballet was far too important an institution to be allowed to vanish with his death—and he protected it as he thought best.

COLLABORATORS

Above, clockwise from front right: Tanaquil LeClercq, Balanchine, Maria Tallchief, Melissa Hayden, Frederick Ashton, Diana Adams, Janet Reed, Jerome Robbins, Antony Tudor, Nora Kaye

Opposite: With Stravinsky *(top)* and Karinska *(bottom)*

Chapter Seven

The New York City Ballet

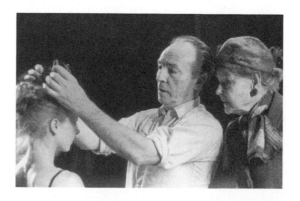

B alanchine's relationships with wives, lovers, dancers tell one side of his story. But from 1948 on, his life was inextricably connected to that of the New York City Ballet as an institution, and as its nature and its fortunes changed, his did as well.

In 1948, postwar New York was a city bursting with energy and the heady excitement of finding itself "the capital of the world," its status confirmed in a geopolitical sense by the presence of the United Nations. But the cultural situation was more nuanced. Europe was still only beginning to recover after the defeat of Germany, yet America—despite the sophistication that the influx of wartime refugees had brought it—still thought of itself as culturally inferior. It had Hollywood, yes, and jazz, and Broadway, but popular culture was not yet taken seriously: Lincoln Kirstein, back in the thirties, had been one of the few to recognize the genius of such figures as Fred Astaire and James Cagney. We had symphony orchestras, opera, museums, but they were all in the European tradition. In New York there were a few adventurous publishing houses, some distinguished "little" magazines, the Museum of Modern Art (where intellectual young guys went to

see movies like Carl Dreyer's *The Passion of Joan of Arc*—and to encounter like-minded girls), a few small movie houses—the Thalia, the Carnegie Hall Cinema, the Fifth Avenue Cinema— that played foreign films (*Symphonie Pastorale, The Bicycle Thief*), the bohemia of Greenwich Village, and Modern Dance, which meant Martha Graham. Ballet was the Ballet Russe and Ballet Theatre, star-studded and old hat. And then along came Ballet Society and the New York City Ballet.

It's hard to grasp, from today's perspective, how provocative, challenging, *special* City Ballet was back then. To go to the City Center and soak up Balanchine's dances and dancers was to be part of a very small elite; the theater was often half empty, despite the popular prices that were part of the mission of this peculiar and uncomfortable theater that belonged to the city and was unabashedly nonprofit. Balanchine, despite his great achievements— from *Apollo, Prodigal Son,* and *Serenade* to *Concerto Barocco, The Four Temperaments,* and *Symphony in C*—was still considered something off to one side. "We happy few" prided ourselves on getting the point; a large part of the dance world, led by the *Times*'s John Martin, was in opposition, although we did have our own critical voice, Edwin Denby, whose refined and profound judgments and analyses were balm.

The company was also, and perpetually, in dire financial straits. Nobody except Lincoln Kirstein had any money, and his resources were limited. The wolf was usually inside the door, the company bouncing from crisis to crisis, rescued more often than not by the City Center's Morton Baum. None of this bothered Balanchine—

he had never been interested in money. When he had it, he spent it or gave it away; when he didn't, he assumed it would turn up. (This carefree attitude, remember, had tormented Danilova back in the Diaghilev days; she wanted to be sure the rent would be paid.) But Balanchine was also practical—he understood survival. He didn't believe in stars, but he made Tallchief a star (her talent and determination helped). He was extending the language of classical ballet in works like *The Four Temperaments* and *Agon,* but when the company needed hits, he came up with *Firebird, Swan Lake, Nutcracker, Stars and Stripes.* And he encouraged Jerome Robbins, who he knew could make hits, too. ("I let Jerry have whatever he wants," he once said to me; "the best dancers, the rehearsal time. He makes hits. Audiences like.") It's hard to know whether, at this time, he was imagining the great establishment institution City Ballet was to become, but he and Kirstein behaved from the start as if what they were doing had a big future.

Perhaps it was the success of *Firebird* that emboldened Kirstein to reach for his most passionate goal, a season at London's Covent Garden. Balanchine had been there in March 1950 staging *Ballet Imperial* (for Margot Fonteyn), and its success convinced the opera house's general adminstrator to offer Balanchine's company a contract for a five-week season in July. It was what Kirstein had dreamed of, but, he writes, "I was apprehensive; England meant so much. . . . One appearance at Covent Garden was a culmination, beyond which there could be nothing: on this I staked everything. It was ridiculous exaggeration. . . . I was not rational; as Frances Hawkins [then the company man-

ager] wisely diagnosed: 'He's not crazy, he's hysterical.'" In the event, victory was not absolute, but it was real. This was in no way the unalloyed triumph that England's Sadler's Wells Ballet had scored in America the year before, but it raised the company's estimation both in its own eyes and in the eyes of the world. Soon City Ballet would be performing across America. And as its wings spread, critical reaction began to change as well. Even John Martin was coming around.

Further foreign tours confirmed that the company was being seen as a serious contender. Kirstein reports that on opening night in Barcelona, in 1952, when the curtain fell on *Symphony in C* the dancers were accorded "the supreme and rare tribute that Barcelona shows to admired artists: a flight of doves flies from every direction over the entire audience. . . . Eight minutes by my watch, the audience applauded the dancers who had by now almost stiffened 'to attention'; Balanchine was visibly moved."

It seems likely, though, that Balanchine's greatest satisfactions through these first years came from the challenging music he was able to explore—Schoenberg, Ives, Hindemith, Webern—and from an influx of superior dancers. He was also gratified that the school was now siphoning first-rate dancers into the company, so that the future would not have to depend on dancers from outside—dancers whom he would have to retrain. Allegra Kent, Jacques d'Amboise, and Edward Villella were harbingers of that phenomenon. And it was the existence of the school that helped make possible *Nutcracker,* the first of Balanchine's ballets to bring children on stage the way he himself had been brought on at the Maryinsky.

From the beginning of his work on *Nutcracker,* he understood that it must be both domestic and magical—the contrast was the heart of the ballet. And he sensed that the magical tree that grows and grows was the crux of the spectacle. As always, he did not hesitate to spend money when it was essential. The budget for *Nutcracker* expanded like the tree itself, and as usual, the money was found. When others fretted about costs, Balanchine would say, "Tell Baum it will only be half as much. The production will get back the money, and he will be happy." His steady grasp of the realities was paying off. One public acknowledgment of his ascendancy was the appearance of his picture on the cover of *Time* magazine the week before *Nutcracker* opened, just as another sign would be Bernard Taper's *New Yorker* profile a few years later. Balanchine was definitely now accepted as a major artist, even if the general public was not yet flocking to the City Center.

Despite the predictable ups and downs of the company's affairs, Balanchine continued as always, apparently unperturbed by crisis or setback. (Only the tragedy of LeClercq really shook him.) It was Kirstein who inevitably worried, always dreaming up new ways to advance City Ballet's fortunes, coming up with ideas and projects—some brilliant, some unrealistic—on which he placed exaggerated importance. The relationship between the two men was complicated—Kirstein in awe of, and endlessly supportive of, Balanchine's genius; Balanchine consistently appreciative and polite. But there was never great personal warmth between them. Kirstein was first and foremost an intellectual, a man of ideas and of words, whose close connections tended to be with writers and artists (and men of influence, like Rockefeller). Despite his dom-

inating presence and powerful personality and temperament, he was emotionally both volatile and fragile, increasingly a victim of a serious bipolar condition. Balanchine had his old pals from Russia, those of his colleagues he could relax with, and his women. He cooked, he gardened, and—central to his life—he had music. Whereas Kirstein had less interest in food than anyone I've ever known—he didn't seem to notice what he was eating—and he was far more interested in art than in music. The two leaders of City Ballet were an odd couple, and Kirstein suffered from feeling that Balanchine didn't really care for him. Lucia Davidova commented, "In spite of their wonderful association, they were never close to each other. Let's say they didn't speak the same language. Once or twice when Lincoln was inviting George for dinner, he'd say to me, 'Come along, it'll be easier for me.' They needed each other, but they never felt on the same ground, somehow."

But can Balanchine be said to have had *any* close friends? Various people suggest that he didn't, and that he didn't need or want them. From early on, Danilova noted, "George was a loner. . . . All his life he was creating ballets—he never really had a personal life apart from the theatre." Igor Youskevitch: "I understood Felia Doubrovska's comment that you could not be chummy with Balanchine. He was a person you could not get too close to . . . we never got to feel 'this is my friend.'" Natalie Molostwoff remarked that he would lose interest in a particular group of friends and move on to another: "He needed change." And yet he was extraordinarily loyal—never turning his back on people from the past, looking after them, always generous with

attention, money, even with his ballets. But one can be good-hearted and good-natured toward others without having strong feelings for them. "He was incapable of really giving in depth," Marie-Jeanne believed; "there was some sort of insecurity there." Dimitriev told Kirstein that Balanchine was "Georgian, heartless." Kirstein echoed that, saying to interviewers that George was "Georgian—like Stalin," even "sinister." And on a calmer note, to Taper, "He seems as soft as silk, but he's as tough as steel." Buckle believed that Balanchine apparently "never felt the need for close friendship with another man . . . both Dimitriev and Kirstein, who saw him daily for years on end, disclaimed the title of intimate friend."

One close associate, Nancy Lassalle, who observed the two men for forty years, remembers how kind Balanchine was when Kirstein was having one of his periodic breakdowns. "There was the terrible summer of Son of Sam. . . . Lincoln was writing crazy, violent letters to George, cutting words out of newspapers and pasting them together to disguise his authorship. George would come over to the school where Lincoln had his office and try to calm him down and help him. You could sense his sympathy." Lassalle also believes that Kirstein increasingly felt himself superfluous—that Balanchine was no longer interested in his ideas and was merely polite about them; and that it was when new ballets were being prepared with which he had little or nothing to do that Kirstein's manic phases were likely to erupt. (Several times, early on, he had to be institutionalized; later, Lithium was able to keep him stable.) In my dealings with Balanchine, I noticed that he would go out of his way to refer certain issues to

Kirstein, but Kirstein was convinced, again, that this was only politeness. Once in the seventies, during some now totally forgotten crisis, Balanchine asked me to ask Lincoln whether a small group of us could meet at his house to discuss the problem. When I proposed this to Lincoln, he shouted that George didn't really mean it; that, in fact, I had invented the whole idea out of kindness to him—to make him feel wanted. This, of course, was in the midst of one of his manic periods, but it suggests what he really felt— that Balanchine had no use for him. And possibly by then that was the case. The dancer Richard Tanner remembers, "By the time I arrived in the company [in 1971], Lincoln Kirstein had a very strange role. He felt exiled to the school, where he had an office. I'd overhear him say things to Balanchine like, 'I never see you.'"

Kirstein, in his book *Thirty Years,* makes it clear what he thought his contributions to the company were—and weren't:

> I've never once in forty-five years suggested to Balanchine either a morsel of music, or the casting of a particular dancer in a ballet, new or old. I have never attempted to arrange scheduling of repertory or tried to project or limit the cost of any new work. I've had nothing to do with price policy in subscription or box-office sales. I've never voiced disagreement over individual dancers, their arrival, presence, or departure. While I have admired a few contemporary painters and sculptors, I have never proposed any as collaborators after Pavel Tchelitchev's abdication from theater. I knew it was hopeless; Balanchine's imagination is less visual than plastic. . . . It has

been suggested I was a kind of public-relations something-or-other. It is true that I've written down what Balanchine suggested or what I've understood him to have said.

This is somewhat disingenuous. Kirstein was certainly involved with various artistic decisions—he was, for instance, a moving force (with Baum) behind the decision to stage *Nutcracker*; he was the bridge to Martha Graham when the two choreographers collaborated on *Episodes,* and was instrumental in bringing works by Merce Cunningham, Frederick Ashton, and other choreographers into the repertoire; and he pushed Balanchine into taking certain boys from the school into the company—but it fairly represents what he believed his role had been. When he comes to stating what his positive contributions were, he focuses on only one: "I take credit for the choice of design of the State Theater with Nelson Rockefeller's subvention from Albany, and for contriving that Philip Johnson design it." This neglects to mention his central participation in the entire Lincoln Center project from first to last. And it leaves out something that was as important as the State Theater to the entire Balanchine enterprise: the extraordinary financial support for the school and the company that Kirstein procured from the Ford Foundation through proselytising Mac Lowry, at that time a power in the foundation. In 1963 more than 7.5 million dollars were given to ballet in the United States, and the company and school were awarded well over half the entire amount. This highly public vote of confidence inevitably situated Balanchine as the pivotal figure

of classical dance in America. (One immediate happy outcome of the grant: The foundation insisted that he accept a salary—he had never had one—and, after asking whether he could use some of the money on a secretary, he was able to take on Barbara Horgan, who had joined the staff a decade earlier as an assistant to Betty Cage and would go on to become Balanchine's closest and most trusted aide, eventually the executor of his estate and the head of the Balanchine Trust and Balanchine Foundation.)

As for the State Theater, moving there was a determining factor in the transformation of City Ballet from a revolutionary enterprise to an acknowledged kingdom. Or to put it another way, from a ma-and-pa store to an official institution. Now Balanchine would have the large stage he had always wanted, in a theater built to his specifications. (He couldn't have known that the acoustics would prove to be a perpetual thorn in everyone's side.) Things did not begin smoothly, however. When he realized that the orchestra pit would hold only thirty-five musicians—the theater was still under construction—he issued one of his rare ultimatums. Kirstein: "Concrete had been poured, but early one morning Balanchine chanced into the auditorium, crowded with forests of scaffolding, to stage one of the most moving and effective solos of his career. After his immediate threat to withdraw our company from further tenancy if the orchestra pit remained straitjacketed, power drills were brought to double the space, so that it can now, with discomfort, hold some seventy men."

One result of the move to the new theater was that a number of ballets had to be reconfigured to take advantage of, or accommodate themselves to, the larger stage area. Some large ballets

benefited markedly from the more spacious circumstances—*Nutcracker, A Midsummer Night's Dream. Symphony in C,* made for the huge stage at the Paris Opéra, finally had enough room—at the City Center, it was always being crowded into the wings. Other ballets suffered: To my mind *Orpheus, La Valse,* and *Divertimento No. 15* in particular have never looked as comfortable at the State Theater as they did at the City Center.

The new theater also made possible ballets on a scale that wouldn't have been possible at the old. The first was *Don Quixote,* a piece with which Balanchine never ceased fussing. He worked with the composer, his old friend Nicolas Nabokov, to improve the not very inspiring score; he choreographed new bits, dropped old ones. Every time *Don Quixote* was scheduled, it was a somewhat different ballet—except in one regard: For a long time no one but Suzanne Farrell danced it.

Then, in 1967, came one of City Ballet's greatest successes, the three-part *Jewels.* From a public relations standpoint, it offered two advantages: It could be presented as the world's first three-act "abstract" ballet; and, supposedly inspired by a visit of Balanchine's to Van Cleef and Arpels, it had all the glamour that jewels convey. On the other hand, it could be (and frequently was) dismissed as a gimmick—that is, as three different ballets artificially linked by a glitzy concept; and critics and audiences spent a lot of time arguing over which section was best and which was weakest.

The three parts were "Emeralds," "Rubies," and "Diamonds"; the music was by Fauré, Stravinsky, and Tchaikovsky; the styles were French, American, and Russian. The subtle and nostalgic

"Emeralds" gave extraordinary opportunities to the incomparably musical Violette Verdy; "Rubies" showcased the all-out rompy energy and clarity of Patricia McBride and Edward Villella; "Diamonds" was yet another anointing of Suzanne Farrell as the epitome, and culmination, of the great Maryinsky tradition of ballerinadom. Taken together, these three ballets—or, if you prefer, these three acts of one ballet—crystallized much of what Balanchine understood about his art. The success of the piece was cannily analyzed by the Balanchine aficionado Robert Garis:

> Unquestionably a major work, but I admire it also because it is a big hit and was meant to be: I like being reminded again of the supreme theatrical instinct that links Balanchine with Shakespeare and Mozart as the kind of genius who can obey and even enjoy and want the necessity of pleasing an audience. *Jewels* is a work of genius both as a work of art and as show-business. . . . The unity of *Jewels* is a matter of surface, of appearance; what is being unified, in fact, is your attention during an evening at the theater. But then that's the aim of all theatrical art. And underneath the expert packaging are three superb new Balanchine ballets.

Yes, and Balanchine's genius extended to knowing just how well these three works went together. (At one point, Melissa Hayden tells us, there was going to be a fourth section, "Sapphires," for her and Arthur Mitchell.)*

---

* *Jewels* provides another example of Balanchine's recycling of ideas. Leonor Fini's notes on the watercolor maquettes for *Le Palais de cristal*, exactly twenty years earlier, read: "Couleurs pour chacque mouvement . . . bijoux [jewels] . . . Premier rouge, rubis . . . Deux noir, diamants noirs . . . Trois émerauds . . . Quatre blanc, perles . . ."

Jewels crowned the success of the State Theater. Later would come the three-act *Coppélia* that Balanchine staged with Danilova (Swanilda had been one of her most famous roles), and *Union Jack* (for America's bicentennial), and, in 1977, the tremendous hit *Vienna Waltzes*. The State Theater was grander, more impersonal than the eccentric City Center, and the audience was growing both larger and perhaps less personally involved. Lincoln Center, the State Theater, the acceptance of ballet as an essential element of "high culture," the famous "dance explosion," the idea of subscription series to sell each season—all these combined to institutionalize the company. Yet it went on being run the same old personal way. Balanchine made his ballets, taught company class, stood in the wings downstage-right every night; Betty Cage, Eddie Bigelow, and Barbara Horgan provided management; Kirstein hovered. For the most part the board of directors did what Kirstein had always intended it to do: Support Balanchine in all his endeavors, and keep hands off. (My own involvement in management, as I have said, came about simply because there weren't enough working hands to get everything done.) The school was pollinating the company with superb new dancers. And Balanchine had found people in public television—Emile Ardolino, Merrill Brockway, Judy Kinberg—with whom he could comfortably work to carry his art to a larger public than could ever be accommodated at the State Theater. He was the recipient of New York City's Handel Medallion and the Kennedy Center Honors. In his sixties, with the criticisms of his ballets as being abstract and cold more or less a thing of the past, Balanchine was universally recognized as a supreme genius and the greatest figure in the international world of dance.

WITH ANDREI

Left: As boys

Below: As men

Chapter Eight

Back to Russia

In 1962, two years before the move to Lincoln Center, Balanchine led City Ballet on its first trip to the Soviet Union, an experience freighted for him with both meaning and anxiety. There
was satisfaction in returning to the country of his birth and training and in showing it what he had accomplished. But this was also
a return home, and about his home he must have been sorely con-
flicted. From 1924, when he left Russia for the West, he had been
surrounded by Russian friends—from Milstein and Horowitz and
Vernon Duke and Dimitriev and all the Diaghilev Russians (to
say nothing of his first two wives) to the musicians and teachers at
the school. He ate in Russian restaurants, cooked Russian food,
drank Russian vodka—and, of course, worshipped Tchaikovsky
and Stravinsky, Pushkin and Tolstoy ("Read the Sermon on the
Mount and *War and Peace* and you'll understand everything," he
told Frederic Franklin). He was also a devout and practicing
member of the Orthodox Church. But apparently he felt none of
the sentimental nostalgia about Russia that so many émigrés express, no longing to be back in the scenes of his youth. In fact, as

quickly as he could he became an American citizen, and from the time a cousin of Tallchief's gave him an American Indian silver-and-turquoise bracelet, he enjoyed wearing Western garb, particularly the string ties that cowboys once sported. His favorite television shows were Westerns.

When Mac Lowry asked him whether he felt alien when he first arrived in America, he said, "No, I never felt that I was a stranger here, you know. I always wanted to be American. I couldn't even speak English at that time, but I really wanted to be American." Tallchief told me, "He saw an Astaire movie when he was in England, and he said, 'That's where I want to be.'" She has written about how *The Four Temperaments* "is steeped in George's contemplation of Astaire. As a result, it marked a new beginning, a conscious departure from the Maryinsky for him. . . . I also believe Astaire was in the back of George's mind when he worked on *Theme and Variations* and *Palais de cristal*. . . . His body moved just the way George wanted his dancers' bodies to move." In 1978, when both men were receiving Kennedy Center Honors, Balanchine was asked, "Have you met Mr. Astaire?" "Oh, no, no, no, no!" (They did eventually meet.) George, Tallchief says, was extremely shy. He was equally crazy about Ginger Rogers and was awestruck when he met her in Hollywood—until she started talking about Christian Science. (He was also, according to Zorina, "enchanted by Busby Berkeley.")

But obviously America meant more to him than just Rogers and Astaire. First and foremost was its energy and speed. And he particularly loved New York City; it was as if his love for St.

Petersburg—a city that tends to obsess its native-born—had been transferred to a safer, more accommodating place. The Russia of his childhood held him to it, but Communist Russia he hated.

In 1962, on landing at Moscow airport where reporters were waiting for him with the statement, "Welcome to Russia, home of the classical ballet," he famously responded, "Thank you, but America is now home of the classical ballet. Russia is home of the old romantic ballet." (In other words, "Where *I* am is the home of classical ballet.") The Russians were claiming him as their own, recording his arrival with photographers and cameramen, but according to the dancer Patricia Neary (as cited by Buckle), the moment he produced his American passport to make clear that he was not coming *home*, the cameras disappeared. Also present at the airport was his brother, Andrei, whom he had not seen since 1918, forty-four years earlier. Andrei, a well-known and admired composer, had with him his younger son, a pianist, and his daughter, a dancer at Georgia's Tbilisi Opera and Ballet Theater. Balanchine, of course, had never met his nephew and niece.

The emotion of returning to Russia and of reuniting with his family merged with nervousness about the company's reception in Moscow, where they opened at the Bolshoi Theater itself, the first American company ever to appear there. Opening night started coolly, with *Serenade,* but by the last ballet, *Western Symphony* — a deliberate celebration of Balanchine's Americanism—it had turned into a triumph. The second program ended with *Symphony in C,* which, according to John Martin, who was along on the tour, was

the real turning point: "The Bizet work brought forth not only applause throughout and repeated curtain calls at the end but also rhythmic cries of 'Bal-an-chine' until the choreographer was forced to come forward and bow his acknowledgment." Even the ultra-modern *Episodes* was received with "tumultuous favor." And at least three of his dancers—Allegra Kent, Edward Villella, and Arthur Mitchell—were wildly acclaimed everywhere.

Even under normal circumstances the company's first appearance in Russia would have caused Balanchine and the company anxiety. But the circumstances were far from normal. These were the weeks of the Cuban missile crisis, when the world was waiting to see whether nuclear war would break out, and when Americans in Russia might reasonably have expected to find themselves in danger, or at least in a potentially ugly situation. On the contrary: One night when the crisis was at its height, as the performance began the entire audience, thousands strong, rose and started cheering. On the last day in Moscow, October 26, the day Khrushchev admitted that the missiles were already in place in Cuba, Balanchine, John Martin wrote, was "mobbed at the stage door by enthusiastic balletomanes who told him emotionally and in extravagant terms that this was the greatest thing that had ever happened to ballet here." When he and the dancers left the theater for their hotel, the crowds shouted after him, "Come back! Come back! Come back!"

According to Richard Buckle and John Taras, immediately after checking into his hotel in Leningrad, "Balanchine grabbed Natalie Molostwoff and rushed out to show her his old home in Bolshoya

Moskovskaya, which was not far away. He was very emotional." Taras observed how depressed he was. He had lost weight, he wasn't sleeping (he claimed that the telephone in his hotel room rang all night long), and he told Pat Neary that he was sure he was being spied on—that his room and maybe even his clothes were being bugged. Suddenly he decided to fly home to New York for a week, before rejoining the company in Georgia. This must have been the kind of panic attack Janet Reed had noted, and what would be more natural? Not only was he exhausted from the effort of leading the company to Russia while having to appear calm and in control through the tension of the missile crisis, but seeing his brother again, and being back in the city of his childhood and youth, where he had endured such emotional and physical hardships, must have agitated his feelings to an unacceptable level.

He was also concerned about LeClercq, who had been without him much of the preceeding period when the company was touring. Indeed, he had asked Barbara Horgan to keep an eye on her while he was gone. During the week he was in New York he was in high spirits, obviously relieved to be away from the grimness of the Soviet Union and the pressures on him there. Horgan remembers that one night he invited her and her parents to a caviar-and-blini dinner at home, and at some point they began talking about a list of the hundred most famous popular songs which had just run in the *Daily News*. Balanchine came up with the list, and they sang all hundred of them—he knew every one. "I still remember him at the piano that night," she recalls, "sitting with his legs crossed like a lounge lizard and singing 'My Funny

Valentine' in flawless English." (The next day, when she compli-
mented him on his lack of accent, he told her that it was Larry
Hart—who had written the lyrics for "My Funny Valentine" and
whom he adored—who had taught him English during their
musical-comedy days.)

This happy interlude restored his equilibrium and prepared him
for the final stretch of the tour. When he rejoined the company in
Tbilisi, his family was there in full force: Andrei, Andrei's wife,
their daughter, and their elder son. Molostwoff told Taper that at
a dinner at Andrei's, despite the warmth between the brothers,
there was prolonged embarrassment when Andrei played records
of his music for his famous big brother. Balanchine just sat there
with his head in his hands, saying nothing. Afterward, when she
asked Balanchine, "Would it have hurt you so much to make some
small compliment about his music?" he answered remorsefully, "I
couldn't. I just couldn't." (Andrei's younger son, Georgi, touchingly
insisted to me recently in St. Petersburg that this wasn't true—that
his uncle really *had* appreciated his father's music.)

To most people Balanchine was silent about his family
through the years that followed his separation from them when he
was fourteen. Tallchief reports that "he revered his father, Meliton,
and missed him terribly. A framed photograph of Meliton stood on
the desk in our bedroom opposite our bed." He never spoke about
his mother, she says, and about Andrei said only that he wasn't a
very good composer. Diana Adams said that he never talked about
his family at any length, but she felt he cared a lot about his
mother. "When he spoke of her, it was with great reverence. It
wasn't very often, but you got the feeling that she had been impor-

tant to him, more than anybody else in the family. When he went to Russia, he wasn't even terribly interested in his brother. Everybody thought he should be, but he wasn't." Karin von Aroldingen says that he never mentioned his mother to her, but spoke of his fondness for his sister. Danilova, who had known his parents, says that his mother "was sweet"; that George always kept a picture of his father with him; that his sister, Tamara, was "not talented"; and that after his parents left him in St. Petersburg, whereas "Others would talk about their families . . . he did not." Yet she told Moira Shearer that to the end of his life, he had "*la tendresse pour sa mère.*" Geva remarks that at the time they married, George had no one. "He had been cut off from his family for years, and though lately they had begun to exchange letters, there was no real bond."

In 1937 Balanchine was teaching in the studio. According to Ruthanna Boris, Lincoln Kirstein came into the room, placed a telegram on the piano, and went out. Balanchine paid no attention to it until class was over. Then he picked it up, read it, "and turned to stone." Saying nothing, he left it on the piano and went away. Boris read it—it had a black border, and it said that his father had died.

Balanchine's mother died in March 1959, only three years before the Russian tour. Buckle points out that "the extent to which he had been cut off from his family may be measured by the fact that his brother Andrei's cable was addressed to the Metropolitan Opera House"—where he had not worked for twenty years. On the day the telegram finally reached him at the City Ballet offices, Barbara Horgan ran into him at the elevator and told him how sorry she was about his mother's death. He said to her, "That's all

right. When someone close to you dies, it's one more person that you have in heaven on your side." Lucia Davidova urged him "to write a nice letter to your brother." When she asked him weeks later if he had done it, Balanchine responded, "No. I just could not bring myself to write."

He had been close to his sister, but she disappeared in Leningrad during the war. He told Volkov, when they were discussing Marie and Fritz, the children in his *Nutcracker,* "I had a sister, too. I was a bit older [actually he was younger], but we never fought. I was a quiet child, and she, too, was peace-loving." One account has it that she was killed during a German air raid; another, that she died trying to escape the siege of the city. He didn't learn the details of his father's death until Andrei was able to relate them when they finally met, twenty-five years after the event. When he married Zorina, he wrote to his mother, "asking for your parental blessing." In this letter, which was in Andrei's possession and was translated for Buckle, Balanchine also asked for Georgian herbs "which are used in making *kharso* [meat soup] and other dishes. And send me the recipe for making *satsivi* [cold chicken with walnuts]. I love cooking myself." He also asked for a *boorka*—a felt coat—and offered to send money for it, and money to Andrei so he can "have his ballet copied out."

Among his possessions when he died were several heavily creased letters from his mother, written in 1935. He's "her dear sonny"; he's "Georgik"; he's "Gogi." She's received a money order from him (for fifty dollars—"This lasted a month and a half."); Andrei has dedicated a new piano concerto to him; Andrei's wife has gone "with the little one" to the country. She would have

valued a letter from her "dear, sweet" Georgik even more than a money order; she wants to hear about his health.

According to her grandson Georgi, his grandmother, who was half German and all Petersburger, was very religious and passionately interested in the arts. Although she lived out her life in Georgia, and understood Georgian, she refused to speak it. And, he remembers, she was always talking about "Georgik" and poring over a box of old family photographs she had brought from Petersburg. It was not only George who suffered from their forty-year separation.

There was no communication with Russia during the war, and afterward Balanchine tried to send food packages, but as the cold war progressed, he was afraid of compromising the family by writing. Even so, it's difficult to believe that over a period of so many years, some arrangement couldn't have been made for a reunion or for more regular correspondence. If to many of his colleagues he never mentioned his family at all, to others there were occasional glancing or quizzical comments. To Frederic Franklin, with whom he spent a good deal of time during the extended Ballet Russe tours of the early forties, he never once referred to his parents, and only once to Andrei: "My brother was a musician." "That's it," Franklin emphasized. And once, out of nowhere, Balanchine said, "I had a letter from my sister." "What? After all this time?" "Maybe it's *not* my sister." Franklin's conclusion: "I feel he was at bottom a very lonely man."

Balanchine as a child had been abandoned—not once but twice. At nine he was deposited at the Maryinsky School and left

there, never really to be absorbed back into the life of the family. Then, when he was fourteen, his family moved away, leaving him on his own. There is no way that a sensitive boy, strongly attached to his mother, would not be damaged by such an abandonment. And it would be recapitulated throughout his life: All his wives, he was to say, left him, rather than the other way around. The anguish he experienced over his rejection by the two women he seems to have been most deeply in love with—Vera Zorina and Suzanne Farrell—can be seen as an echo of the grief he experienced at this early time. Until almost the end of his life, he avoided anything like a family situation: Women, yes; real wives, no; children, never. He once said to Janet Reed, "I can stand any amount of work. I can work endlessly. But I can't cope with human relationships, difficult relationships." And it was when he tried, Reed remarks, that he had his panic attacks.

But how in his dislocated childhood would he have learned to engage deeply with others? Clever Danilova speculated to Taper about the time when they were living together: "I think, perhaps, he had not learned in those days how to love another human being. Perhaps if he had not been separated so much from his family, he might have learned that—and learned not to bury his feelings. And there was all the upheaval of the Revolution we lived through, affecting him and all of us. In a way we were little wild animals. We were forced to bring ourselves up, to improvise our lives—and that left its mark." For years, Tallchief says, he had terrible nightmares, "and when they occurred he'd call out in his sleep in an unfamiliar tongue." She assumed it was Georgian, his first language.

·   ·   ·

Whatever Balanchine's state of mind on being back in Russia and being confronted with what was left of his family after so long a separation, the performances in Georgia were a continuous triumph, and he was being hailed as a world-famous native son (although he had never before set foot in Georgia). He took Molostwoff with him on a pilgrimage to the town of Kutaisi, where his father was buried and where his older half-brother Apolon lived. Instead of being restful, this reunion involved yet another round of raucous banquets. By the time the company reached Baku, the final date on the tour, the dancers and Balanchine were utterly depleted. Buckle (via Taras) reports:

> A huge party was given in the hotel ballroom on the night before they left, and everybody got drunk. Shaun O'Brien put on his new Russian musquash hat and removed his pants. When the party broke up, dancers began to visit one another's rooms. Shaun called on Betty [Cage] and Natalie [Molostwoff], to find the latter ready for the morning flight, fully dressed and wearing her earrings, but fast asleep on top of her bed. Then Balanchine came in and sat down. He said, "Well, I suppose now the tour is over everybody's little love affairs will be over too. All except mine—I never had any." Shaun remarked, "You could have, if you wanted to." "No," said Balanchine, "nobody loves me." Then Shaun did something he would never had dared to do if he were sober; he ran to Balanchine, sat on the arm of his chair, patted him and exclaimed, "But we all love you!" Balanchine looked him in the eye without expression and said, "Where are your pants?"

LATER YEARS

Above: Rehearsing
Karin von Aroldingen

Right: Backstage with
Madame Sophie
Pourmel, costume
mistress of the New
York City Ballet

B alanchine's last dozen or so years were on the whole the calmest and steadiest of his life. The company's artistic peak, and his moment of greatest acclaim, came with the 1972 Stravinsky festival, which he mounted to honor the composer on the first anniversary of his death and what would have been his ninetieth birthday. To celebrate the Master—"Mr. Stravinsky provides me with wonderful time, and I like to swim in it. . . . He was like Einstein—nobody like him"—he devoted a weeklong festival to him, presenting not only the old ballets, beginning with *Apollo,* but a slate of new pieces, made by himself, Robbins, Taras, and others. Ignoring the extra cost ($130,000), he closed the theater for a week of rehearsals—there was no other way to prepare some thirty ballets in so short a time. (Kirstein compared the rehearsal period to "a miniature Normandy landing.") In an astonishing tour de force, he himself created three major works while supervising the entire enterprise: *Duo Concertant, Symphony in Three Movements,* and *Stravinsky Violin Concerto*—this last, he was to

say, the one work of his he wouldn't change a step of. In the wake of the festival, the critic Richard Poirier wrote in the *Atlantic Monthly*, "In the history of ballet, Balanchine at New York's State Theater is equivalent to Shakespeare at London's Globe." I suspect that in Balanchine's mind, the Stravinsky festival was the culminating—the most gratifying—event of his artistic lifetime.

The company was now on steady financial ground, and he could do just about what he chose. There would be a Ravel festival, a Tchaikovsky festival, another Stravinsky festival. This is the period of the company blockbusters *Union Jack* and *Vienna Waltzes,* of *Chaconne* (Farrell and Martins at their most Olympian) and *Ballo della Regina* (delighting in the virtuoso speed and allegro attack of Merrill Ashley), and of two final masterpieces: *Robert Schumann's "Davidsbündlertänze"* (1980) and *Mozartiana* (1981). The former used Schumann's piano suite as the arena in which four couples seem to embody aspects of the composer's history and psyche. It would be fruitless to try to pin down these themes explicitly, but one can imagine that Farrell somehow stands for the artist's muse, and von Aroldingen for the loving and despairing Clara, Schumann's faithful wife. At first, *Davidsbündlertänze* looked almost uncertain, as if the dancers weren't sure what they were meant to be doing; the four couples had been taught their passages separately, not as part of a whole. Only after about a year of performances did it suddenly cohere and reveal its bleak yet profoundly moving core. Madness, the death of hope, the destruction of the artist—this is the direction in which Balanchine's mind was tending toward the end of his life.

And yet his final major work, *Mozartiana,* is a celebration—of music, of dance, of life. The music is Tchaikovsky's tribute to Mozart, and the ballet is Balanchine's tribute to them both—it's tempting to read his nature, very loosely, as synthesizing the temperaments of those two geniuses whom he adulated: The generosity and deep pessimism of Tchaikovsky, the merriment and detachment of Mozart. *Mozartiana,* following the Schumann, has an effect comparable to that of the joyous, life-affirming coda to *Don Giovanni* following the passion and turmoil of the opera's dark drama. And it seems fitting that this final work of consequence should have been inspired by Farrell, who was later to write, "It was because this ballet existed that I could survive the death of the man who made it."

The last years of his life, beginning in 1969, were warmed by a new companion—and a new *kind* of companion. In 1962, at the recommendation of Lotte Lenya, he had accepted a young German girl into the *corps de ballet.* She was Karin von Aroldingen, a tall, fair, rather athletic-looking dancer without real classical polish but with absolute determination to improve and prevail. Early on, she married a businessman named Morton Gewirtz, and had a daughter—dancing into the sixth month of her pregnancy and back in class a week after the birth. A month later she rejoined the company, which was on tour, and resumed her career. She was quoted back then as saying, "I am first a dancer, before I am a wife and mother. And I care a lot about my family."

For seven years, von Aroldingen has said, she never spoke to Balanchine, but eventually, on a long plane flight, she dared to approach him with a personal problem and ask for advice. Suddenly they were friends, and eventually they were family. He liked her Germanness, von Aroldingen believes—he had always been drawn to Germany, ever since the escape to Stettin in 1924; perhaps all the way back to his half-German mother and German nurse. He liked her dancing—the opportunities her unconventional look and style, and her complete devotion, offered him—and he made a series of remarkable roles on her: from the carefree girl with the big jump in *Who Cares?* to the sinuous, acrobatic first duet in *Stravinsky Violin Concerto* to the first section of *Vienna Waltzes* (no one else in the company understood old-world waltzing the way she did) to the blazing attack of her *Union Jack* to the robotic precisions of *Kammermusik No. 2* to the loving, nurturing Clara Schumann who cannot, finally, protect her Robert from disintegration and death.

In real life, von Aroldingen became the loving and nurturing woman he had either never sought or never found after his mother's disappearance from his life. (Strangely—or not so strangely—his mother's original name was von Almedingen; she became Vassilyeva after her German father abandoned his family.) She made no unreasonable demands, she enjoyed cooking with him, sharing his spare time (he had always hated the emptiness of weekends and holidays when there was no work to be done), looking after him. And she absorbed him into her family—the first real family he had known since he was nine. In

Morty and Margo Gewirtz, he was at last able to accept the husband and child of a muse. During the company's summer seasons in Saratoga Springs they all shared a house, and they lived close to each other in the Hamptons, where he had been persuaded to buy a small condominium. She was the friend who was his domestic lifeline, just as Barbara Horgan was the friend who was his professional lifeline.

In his seventies Balanchine was assaulted by a series of physical infirmities. He had a triple bypass operation, from which he rebounded amazingly quickly. But then his eyes deteriorated—he had an operation for glaucoma and surgery for cataracts. His balance gave way, which meant that he could no longer demonstrate, either in class or in the studio. As his condition worsened, his behavior grew erratic. Zorina, whom he had invited to participate in the 1982 Stravinsky festival, as the narrator of *Perséphone*, writes: "I began to realize that George was not himself. It was therefore all the more frightening when he screamed one day in total rage during a production meeting: 'Only *I* know what to do—nobody else knows anything!'" He told her, "When I go, never will be another Balanchine—that's finished." Another time he said, "I'm finished. I can't see anymore, I can't hear, and I walk like a drunken man." At rehearsals, she says, she was sometimes afraid to go near him. "At times he looked as if he did not know who I was."

As he grew more and more feeble, it became increasingly evident that something very serious was affecting his health, yet

neither his doctor, Edith Langner, nor his friend the company surgeon, Bill Hamilton, nor experts who were consulted could diagnose the problem. It was not until after his death that traces were discovered in his brain of the rare Creutzfeldt-Jakob disease—a condition that apparently can be communicated to humans from sheep, much the way that "mad cow" disease works. Dr. Robert Wickham, a distinguished urologist who attended him in his last months, recalls that Balanchine "was very much concerned about staying as youthful as possible," and had told him that he had "obtained 'rejuvenation' injections in Switzerland," a treatment popular in European clinics for many years. (At one time such procedures were known as "monkey gland" treatments.) These injections can contain extracts of animal glands "such as testicular tissue," and, Wickham concludes, "It is quite possible that he got Creutzfeldt-Jakob disease by way of these injections."

By the fall of 1982 he was suffering from a series of dangerous mishaps at home—he was no longer leaving his apartment—and eventually it became unsafe for him to stay there, even with constant nursing and the loving attendance of Barbara Horgan, Eddie Bigelow, Karin von Aroldingen and Morty, and others close to him. After a severe fall one evening, he said to Barbara, "You've done all you can and tried everything, but I shouldn't be here. My home is not a hospital." On November 4, he was admitted to Roosevelt Hospital, which he was never to leave. For almost six months he lingered, at first trying to stay abreast of things at the theater, then retreating further and fur-

ther into silence. There was a stream of visitors until the very end. Dancers from the past flew in—from California, from Europe—to see him one last time. Baryshnikov came, bringing spicy Georgian food from a restaurant in Brooklyn; Nureyev was seen kneeling next to his bed, weeping. Geva, Danilova, Tallchief came again and again. The very young Darci Kistler, his final discovery, whom he adored, insisted on seeing him, and told Buckle, "Mr. B. recognized me, and he listened to me." The last time Tallchief saw him, she said, she and her husband "entered the dimly lit room and music was playing. Balanchine was tapping the fingers of both hands against each other. I asked, 'What are you doing, George?' And he replied, 'You see, I'm making steps.'"

At the end it was only Karin he wanted, and she stayed with him day after day, holding his hand. He died on April 30, 1983, at four in the morning. The hospital called Barbara Horgan, and it was her sad duty to inform Karin, Lincoln Kirstein, and the others closest to him.

It was a Saturday, with both afternoon and evening performances scheduled. At the matinee, von Aroldingen managed to dance *Kammermusik No. 2*—Peter Martins had asked her if she wanted to dance, and she knew that she had to. That evening, Suzanne Farrell went on in *Symphony in C*. Martins was hardly dancing any longer, most of his time devoted to running the company, but when she asked him to dance with her that night, he readily agreed. Appropriately, it was Lincoln Kirstein who, fifty years earlier, had brought Balanchine to America, who

spoke to the audience from the stage, saying to us, "I don't have to tell you that Mr. B. is with Mozart and Tchaikovsky and Stravinsky." If any thought could have helped, it would have been that.

The funeral took place at the small Russian Orthodox cathedral of Our Lady of the Sign. More than a thousand mourners stood grieving. It was very crowded, and airless. Of his five wives, only Zorina, who was abroad, was absent. Perhaps those who shared Balanchine's deeply religious nature found solace in the long and bewildering service, but I'm sure that for most of those present, the overwhelming emotion was that of loss. Of his ex-wives, his dancers past and present, his colleagues, friends, and admirers, there can have been very few who were not looking anxiously toward the future. Balanchine had said, "We are now in this period when people say, 'Oh, my God, what will happen when you go?' But everything goes. . . . It wouldn't be any good fifty years from now to do what we do now. It will be something else." But this philosophic approach was of little comfort. Everyone there understood how fragile an art ballet is. If New York City Ballet and the Balanchine repertory were to disintegrate without him, the supreme artistic experience of their lives would be over. Who cared, at that moment, what it would all be like in fifty years? As John Taras was to write, "Now that he's gone, it's another world."

PORTRAITS OF MR. B

Chapter Ten

The Man

In the hard days after Diaghilev's death, in the early unsettled time in America, even in the first years of City Ballet, had Balanchine foreseen that he would reach so preeminent a position or command a company of such unique brilliance? It's unlikely that he ever articulated even to himself so grandoise an ambition (although Kirstein certainly might have, for him), but one has the impression that he always had a sense of where he was heading and what his capacities were. Apart from Petipa and (early) Fokine, there were not many choreographers he respected. Of his contemporaries, Frederick Ashton was the only possible rival, and they had a tense relationship, defined by a desire for approbation on Ashton's part and a certain hauteur on Balanchine's. (Julie Kavanagh, in her superb biography of Ashton, quotes from a review he wrote of Taper's book: "George Balanchine, a contemporary and colleague of mine, is the choreographer that I most admire in the world. . . . All the Russian fairies must have gathered at his christening to bestow on him all his great gifts." Whereas, according to Kirstein, Balanchine never took Ashton very seriously because of his lack of proper musical

training, and because "he deplored [Ashton's] kind of lightness and feigned silliness.") He obviously held Martha Graham in some regard, since he invited her to participate in the two-part *Episodes* in 1959, but the Graham connection, like the invitation to Merce Cunningham to stage his *Summerspace* for the company, reflected Kirstein's interests, not Balanchine's. He respected Robbins as a junior partner; allowed several of Antony Tudor's works into the repertory when Tudor himself, together with Hugh Laing, Nora Kaye, and Diana Adams, joined the company; and encouraged many of his younger colleagues to try their hand at choreography—he was impressed enough with Peter Martins's first ballet, *Calcium Light Night,* to fold it into his own *Ivesiana.*

In private, however, he was not reluctant to express his opinion of other choreographers. The knives were often out. Once, when I mentioned to him that the night before I had suffered through a performance of John Cranko's *Eugene Onegin,* with its patched-together Tchaikovsky score, he said, "You know why that one die?" (Cranko had died young, of a heart attack.) "Tchaikovsky up in heaven looked down and saw that ballet and went to God and said, 'Get that one!'" As far back as the pre-America days, he had been blunt. Boris Kochno remembers that when someone asked him what he thought of other choreographers, he answered, "And who *are* the other choreographers?" He could be equally dismissive of composers, from Prokofiev and Rachmaninov, both of whom he disliked personally, to Shostakovich ("a dreadful composer; he wrote like a peasant, a

muzhik") to Bartók and Dvořák ("horribly overrated") to Sibelius ("now nobody plays him; his music is a disaster").

His security about his place in dance history, combined with his conviction that he was in the hands of fate, made it possible for him to confront moments of crisis imperturbably. Kirstein was to say that the biggest crisis the company ever faced was the orchestra strike of 1976—deliberately timed for the run of *Nutcracker,* in order to do the greatest possible damage to the box office. Balanchine met this setback with his usual aplomb. On the one hand, he was eager to get back to work; on the other, he was resigned to whatever might happen. On another occasion, an orchestra negotiation went on and on until the audience was already coming into the theater for the opening night of a new season. When several of us rushed up to his fourth-floor office at about seven-thirty to tell him that matters had been concluded satisfactorily, we found him quietly sipping champagne with Barbara Horgan: There was nothing he could do to help matters, so why get agitated? If we opened, we opened; if not, not. There would be other openings.

But when there *was* something he could do to deal with a difficulty, he was on it like a flash. (I observed that the words "We have a problem" always instantly stimulated him.) A memorable example: During the 1976 orchestra strike the dispute had been submitted to arbitration and been moved to the World Trade Center. (We had been in discussions for almost six months.) One morning, after hours of sitting around waiting to meet with the orchestra committee, all of us on the management

team ran out of dimes to use in the public telephones—this was before cell phones, of course—but were afraid to leave the building to get more, in case we were suddenly summoned to the bargaining table. Eddie Bigelow used his last dime to leave a message for George Michelmore, the company's orchestra contractor, to bring dimes, and plenty of them. An hour later Balanchine burst into the room with a bag of dimes, asking, "Am I in time?" They had given the message to the wrong George, and he had assumed that the dimes were somehow crucial to the negotiations. He was so grateful to have been given a useful job to do that no one had the heart to disillusion him.

Another scene: The Tchaikovsky festival of 1981 was notable for an amazing backdrop that had been commissioned from Philip Johnson for the entire celebration. It was a gigantic assemblage of translucent plastic tubes strung together and hung from the top of the stage, and it was very beautiful when properly lit. But on the day it was being installed—which was the day the festival was to begin—all was chaos. One of the very large, heavy tubes crashed to the stage, narrowly missing a stagehand, who would have been seriously injured if it had struck him. And then, as the tubes were exposed to the heat of the powerful stage lights, they began to smell (actually, they began to stink). No one knew whether the stage would be ready in time or whether the theater would be habitable. Balanchine sat in the middle of the theater, ignoring the hysteria surrounding him, totally focused on the way Merrill Ashley's *Swan Lake* tiara sat on her head. That was the one thing he could do something about, and he was doing it.

.　.　.

This composure in the face of imminent disaster had been a characteristic of Balanchine's as long as anyone could remember—I present these particular examples only because I happened to witness them. There are countless other stories. People still recall, for instance, his calm on various opening nights when the great costume designer Karinska would arrive at the theater a quarter of an hour before curtain time with the new costumes she had been making and hardly enough time to pin them on the waiting dancers. Again, it was all in the hands of fate—unless his own hands could help fate along. (He was known to pin and sew along with everyone else.)

What he didn't like was theorizing or even explaining. His instructions to his dancers were inevitably expressed either through demonstration or through analogy. Dancer after dancer bears witness to how extraordinary his own dancing was when he taught or coached. Melissa Hayden remembers him teaching Allegra Kent the Swan Queen: "He was in street shoes and he did the part more beautifully than anyone else. . . . He can do anything. His body speaks." Patricia McBride: "He would show everything so beautifully. I felt that I could never do it as beautifully as he could. . . . In 1970 he did the variation in *Who Cares?* for me. He was sixty-five and he did that whole variation, the rhythms, the body, much better than I could." His women dancers testify again and again to his profound understanding of pointe work, and of partnering. As for the men, Daniel Duell describes how when Balanchine demonstrated *Apollo*, "He could

get the feeling, the essence of the movement quality, by demonstrating with his arms and his upper body without doing the whole step. You would understand the expressive intent. He'd leave you with the feeling that you could never dance it as beautifully as he did." Edward Villella: "The most wonderful thing was that he was such a great dancer that he would show you and you really didn't need words."

When he did speak about a step or a role, it was with a simple image that would uncannily convey his intentions. Villella, in his autobiography, recalled his experience learning *Prodigal Son*: "Working on the section in which the drinking companions run their fingers up and down the Prodigal's exhausted, nearly naked body as if to strip it further of worldly goods, Balanchine said to them, 'Like mice.' It spoke volumes. It was as if they were going to eat my flesh, and it made me cringe." Again, "In the ballet's central pas de deux, a difficult moment occurs when the Siren sits on the Prodigal's neck, without holding on to anything for support. Balanchine said to the dancer, Diana Adams, 'Well, it's like you're sitting and smoking a cigarette,'" and, commented Villella, "that remark recalled to me images of models in old cigarette advertisements. I could see the way she would be sitting, the way she'd pose, and the way I would have to balance her." At another moment, when the Siren steps off the Prodigal's legs as he lowers them to the floor, Balanchine said, "Good. You lower her like elevator." Most crucial was Balanchine's saying, "Icons. You know, dear. Byzantine icons." It was the key to the role for Villella. (To Victor Castelli, to whom Balanchine was teaching the last scene in which the Prodigal

crawls home, he simply said, "Dear, just pretend you're Jewish!")

Paul Taylor, whom Balanchine borrowed from Martha Graham for the *Episodes* collaboration, wrote about the final day of rehearsal, "Since the solo seems to be about something, yet its subject is a mystery to me, I ask Mr. B if there is any particular way that it's to be performed. 'Umm,' he answers, nose fidgeting and sniffing out a proper image. 'Is like fly in glass of milk, yes?' The picture was perfect. The convoluted dance, resembling the buzzing circles of something subhuman, caught within a deadly vortex of its own making, seemed to be an epigram about self-ordained patterns and death."

Rosemary Dunleavy, the company's ballet mistress, remembers how helpful it was when Balanchine was making the finale of *Stravinsky Violin Concerto* that he kept talking to the dancers about the waiters in the Russian Tea Room. "All that walking around—that was all Russian Tea Room waiters," she has said. "Not only was that his imagery, but that's what stays with you. . . . When you say 'Russian Tea Room Waiters' to a dancer, something clicks."

In class he would want the foot at certain times to look almost boneless, not like a joint—"like an elephant's trunk," he would say, "the way an elephant picks a peanut off the floor." (He was to use this image in a very different context when choreographing the Peter Martins–Kay Mazzo *pas de deux* in *Stravinsky Violin Concerto*. Martins: "The final gesture . . . looks almost sentimental: I cover her eyes with one hand as she leans backwards against me and open the other arm out before us. Balanchine's directions to us were 'Make it look like an elephant trunk, and then move

out your hand as if you're asking for money.'") Or, when the leg was extended forward, he would want it rotated "so you can serve a glass of champagne on your heel; as if you're serving your foot." John Clifford, a favorite of Balanchine's, reports him saying things like, "Don't just stand there like a dead fish! Reach for it like you're reaching for a Cadillac!" and, about pointing the feet, "Press like you're pressing on the accelerator of an MG!"

Teaching was the heart and soul of his enterprise—he was frequently quoted as saying that he would be remembered first and foremost as a teacher, not as a choreographer. The school was now firmly in place as the premier training ground for ballet dancers in America. It taught the basics the way he wanted them taught, and he was secure in the competence of his teachers, who through the years included important dancers from his Russian past—Pierre Vladimirov, the *danseur noble* who had been Pavlova's last partner; Anatole Oboukhoff; Doubrovska; and eventually Danilova herself, who taught Petipa variations—and demonstrated in her person (as did Doubrovska) what a ballerina should be. These women were elegant, refined, fastidious, and demanding. They understood, as Balanchine did, that the studio, like the stage, was a sacred place, to be treated with respect. The dancer and teacher Suki Schorer writes, "The only time I recall Mr. B being truly angry came when he discovered a stagehand casually dropping ashes from his cigar on the freshly mopped stage just before a performance. 'Don't you know where you are? You're not in the street! This is not a gutter!' he yelled. 'This is the theater, a place where people *dance*!'"

When students graduated from the school into the company, they had been taught how he wanted them to look—how each step should be produced. They knew how to dance. Company class was for refining and extending what they knew. In some companies daily class is essentially a warm-up period. Balanchine's class was a continuing exploration of details that were important to him. As far back as the late thirties, Mary Ellen Moylan tells us, "He would often focus on a particular step. It might be a *tendu,* it might be a *glissade,* whatever it was that he wished to stress. I think he felt that the other teachers could do the general, well-rounded class, but he would rather impart some specific point to us."

Peter Martins confirms this: "For one hour he will work on three steps, and these will be simple steps, but it is what he gets out of these steps that is important. . . . He'll try a small jump and you'll do it twenty-five times over, and for ten minutes you'll do it very slowly, and then he will increase the speed. After twenty minutes of repeating this step you'll find yourself exhausted, but you'll also have increased your mastery, and your body will have been schooled to do the step perfectly." When Balanchine invited Martins to give company class, "He warned me not to go to class with ten astonishing combinations just to show off my wonderful ideas and how creative I was. 'You aren't there to give them a dance to do, to give them dancing lessons. You are there to make them feel the steps in their own bodies.'"

In her book on Balanchine technique, Schorer, whom Balanchine tapped when she was very young both to give lecture-demonstrations and to teach, parses the way he wanted each step

performed as well as underlining his general principles. "Energy, dynamics, and controlled abandon were more important to him than having every dancer's arm in the same line, because that approach generally demands more constrained, more calculated movement. Remember, 'No polite dancing!'" (In a famous, pithy phrase, "Don't think, dance.") "Even when there is a calmness in Balanchine's ballets," Schorer emphasizes, "there is an energy within that calmness. Calmness doesn't mean lack of energy or life." The key word, always, is "energy," underscored by almost every dancer who has written about him. Energy, clarity, speed, articulation—these are the qualities that identify a Balanchine dancer. And an expressivity that comes from full investment in the steps rather than from emoting. "Don't act. Just do the steps," is a Balanchine mantra. Which doesn't mean that his work doesn't generate the most intense emotions—unless you're dance-deaf, the way some people are tone-deaf.

Today the company's ballet masters and the teachers in the school are for the most part highly experienced ex-Balanchine dancers, though not necessarily from the very top ranks. There is Martins, of course, who heads both the company and the school, and Kay Mazzo, co-chair of the school's faculty, but most of City Ballet's leading dancers of the past are either running companies elsewhere—Helgi Tomasson in San Francisco, Villella in Miami, Farrell in Washington, McBride and her husband, Jean-Pierre Bonnefoux, in Charlotte; Arthur Mitchell in Harlem; Daniel Duell in Chicago; Robert Weiss in Raleigh; Ib Anderson in

Phoenix—or, like Violette Verdy, Allegra Kent, Patricia and Colleen Neary, Jillana, Maria Calegari and her husband, Bart Cook, and John Clifford, they either teach elsewhere or stage and coach Balanchine ballets through the Balanchine Trust. Tallchief was active in Chicago for many years; Francia Russell —another leading stager of his works—and her husband, Kent Stowall, have run Pacific Northwest for more than two decades; Todd Bolender has done the same in Kansas City, and so on. Of the last generation of central Balanchine dancers, only Merrill Ashley and Karin von Aroldingen (both of whom own Balanchine ballets) remain connected to the company.

The lack of input from these key artists represents a severe loss to New York City Ballet, but it is the resulting diaspora of Balanchine dancers that has spread both his repertory and his approach to dancing throughout the Western world. This may seem to echo what happened after Diaghilev's death, when his ex-dancers and choreographers, including Balanchine, carried "the word" everywhere. But there was no single Diaghilev word: Nijinska, Massine, Lifar, Balanchine, Marie Rambert, Ninette de Valois all had different visions and different agendas. Balanchine's death, twenty-odd years ago, has led to *his* word spreading everywhere, through the loyalty and application of his direct heirs. Today Balanchine feeds every important repertory, even though not all the resulting performances necessarily reflect his imperatives: The Kirov, the Bolshoi, Britain's Royal, the Paris Opéra are never going to look like Balanchine-inspired companies or companies that embody the precepts of the School of American

Ballet. Even so, as the work of his immediate predecessors and near contemporaries—Fokine, Massine, Nijinska, et al.—seems to recede into history, Balanchine is more and more left standing alone, a giant figure whose work and influence impose themselves everywhere on the art he loved and transformed.

As for Balanchine himself, he remains a mystery—a word friends and colleagues often applied to him. He was both cool and ardent, sad and full of fun, arrogant and modest, a much-married man who never really wanted a wife, a towering genius who liked to iron and to play solitaire. Let Nathan Milstein, a friend from his youth, have the last word: "Yes, it is likely that Balanchine's ballets will die someday, and that will be a great loss. But George left an inheritance that consists of more than his works. He left his moral example, a considerable legacy: the strength and wholeness of his character; his directness, adherence to principle, and lack of greed. . . . his devotion to his art; his independence of fashion, fame, and trappings of success. . . .

"When I think of Balanchine, I see him again. There he is— a real Russian personality. His face is sharply drawn; his body is lean, trained, flexible. He walks erect, confidently; quickly but without rushing. That impossible Texan string tie dangles from his neck (he has 'regular' ties somewhere, but they're so much trouble). He exudes elegance, energy, joy. That's how I remember him."

Words by George Balanchine

Although Balanchine was famous for many epigrammatic utterances, he was not interested in being a writer. The book that carries his name is *Balanchine's Complete Stories of the Great Ballets,* published in 1954, for which his collaborator, Francis Mason, did all the writing and about which Balanchine was totally hands-off except in regard to his own work. He auditioned Mason by asking him to try one ballet, and Mason chose *Serenade.* "Read it to me," Balanchine said. Then, "Too long. Hopeless. You have to leave something to the imagination. Don't tell names of steps." When Mason came back with a second, much shorter version, the verdict was, "That's okay." About everyone else's ballets, says Mason, Balanchine didn't give a damn: "Francis, I trust you." He wouldn't read the galley proofs, and when he read (or read in) the final book, he had only one comment: "Francis, I have read book. On page [so and so], we are saying Anton Rubinstein, not Arthur Rubinstein." Even so, this useful book, in several editions, stayed in print for decades.

One of the very few bylines I've seen of Balanchine's is in the June 11, 1965, issue of *Life* magazine. The article is called "Mr. B Talks About Ballet" and is illustrated with photographs by Gjon Mili, many of them focused on Balanchine and Suzanne Farrell during the making of *Don Quixote.* The tone is characteristic Balan-

chine, though undoubtedly the piece was prepared with the help of Lincoln Kirstein or Betty Cage. But there can be no question about the authenticity of the views Balanchine expresses on many subjects. In fact, they bear a remarkable similarity to the things he was saying to Kirstein during their first long conversation, in 1933.

I am reprinting it here entire, since as far as I know it has never been available since its initial publication.

Mr. B Talks About Ballet

by George Balanchine

When a person first comes into the ballet he should come and see, come and discover. If you take a person to see a great painting in a gallery—to see a Michelangelo, for instance—he might say, "So what? It's very boring, just a man standing there. What is good about it?" So you say, "You might not see anything in the beginning maybe, but look longer." And if he comes again and again and stares—sure enough, the fifth or sixth time, he will see how beautiful it is, how the air becomes transparent and you can smell it; there is a glow—the space, the hands, everything is fantastically beautiful. And he wants to see more.

It is the same at the ballet. Just come in and stare. Don't listen to anybody, especially not to so-called balletomanes. These slinky people belong to a circle of "connoisseurs" who follow a dancer not because she is good but because she is famous and they want to say, "I know her." Finally they go to her dressing room, she invites them to tea and they instantly become balletomanes. They are as ignorant as before

*Reprinted by permission of the George Balanchine Trust.

and they have bad taste. These balletomanes breed bad taste and mediocrity.

The people who really appreciate ballet come and just look at it and if they don't understand, come back again. It's cheap, at our theater it is cheaper than the movies. Besides, we have a fine 60-man orchestra and we play music rarely played at concerts: Stravinsky, Webern, Hindemith. If you don't want to see what's on the stage, close your eyes and for two dollars you get a beautiful concert.

But if you watch the stage you will see something more beautiful. The ballet is a purely female thing; it is a woman, a garden of beautiful flowers, and man is the gardener. Woman can do without man in the ballet, but man cannot have any ballet company without woman. Male dancers don't like to hear it but I believe it. They are very important as princes and attendants to the queen, but woman is the queen. Ballet is one place where art flourishes because of the woman; woman is the goddess, the poetess, the muse. That is why I have a company with beautiful girl dancers. I believe the same is true of life, that everything man does he does for his ideal woman. You live only one life and you believe in something and I believe in a little thing like that. It has worked so far. It will last me.

Today every child wants to dance just as every child wants to run and jump. Then they hear lovely music—marches, waltzes, music that makes you want to dance. It is in the nature of man to want to dance when he hears music. In old times theater was taboo, theater was a sin. If you wanted to go on the stage, it was almost as if you should be punished. But now, it's like Jimmy Durante said, "Everybody wants to get into the act." Now dancing schools are available and every young mother wants her daughter to dance.

But not her son. There is the idea that boys must be tough, not sissies. To be tough you have to play football; even if you are a sissy, you play football. Nobody knows that you have to be tough to be a

dancer and people don't realize that ballet doesn't make a man a sissy at all—just the reverse.

When boys at our school are 12 they begin to support girls. A boy must touch a girl's hand and exert pressure to balance the girl. The hands must communicate, and the eyes, this is the only communication we have. When we start to teach a boy how to support a girl it has nothing to do with sex, it is purely dance and acrobatics. And yet, dancing with a particular girl, the boy will come home and say, "Hmmm, she has beautiful eyes." And the next time he sees her he says, "Hello, how are you?" You see, already something happens. He has 100% more chance to be a man than if he were not involved with girls.

We used to have no male students at all. But Jacques d'Amboise started with us at the age of 8. He is now married and has four children. And Edward Villella also started at about age 8 and also grew up to be a man. And both of them are good. So our percentage is 200%—100 for each.

The young generation understands it is not sissy anymore and we now have schools for them. Thirty years ago there was little in this country—a couple of touring commercial companies and few dancers. Then, with Hitler, refugees came here and started to teach. Now we have wonderful children coming up. The dancers here have exceptional bodies. You choose them as you would choose horses. There are a lot of horses in the U.S. and when you choose them to run, some are faster and better. We have a wonderful company here; we could have double, three the times the number of dancers we have if we had more money. The English feel they have a fantastic company, too. They are beautifully trained but they prefer lyricism to energy. I like large and energetic movements. It's a little like a sneeze; in Russia I learned to sneeze and make a lot of noise doing it. The English are too polite to really finish the sneeze.

The French are very talented people, very musical. But the really

important thing to them is a good meal. It's difficult to dance after eating a big, wonderful meal. In Italy, because of the opera, they don't treat dancers very well. The opera is always first, symphony second, third the directors, stagehands, chorus. Last of all the lousy dancers.

Russia is different. Ballet has a very high priority and they are proud of it. Russia has lots of energy; that's the way I am. They dance the way I teach.

Back in Russia when I was a boy people really didn't like ballet. Only the Russian nobility were the balletomanes—all those men in the first few rows looking at the beautiful dancers, the same awful cast of people who today scream when a dancer comes on stage and hasn't even done anything yet. But our court didn't care much for the dance. They just wanted to see a story.

In ballet a complicated story is impossible to tell. You cannot use words. You can't dance synonyms. *Swan Lake* is just nothing, except maybe those little swans. The wicked magician brings in a girl who *looks* like the original girl. It's the same ballerina and the whole illusion is lost. In Russia, the balletomanes came to *Swan Lake* to see Kschesinskaya do those 32 *fouettés* on point. She was the only one who could do it then. Today hundreds can do it and they also have much better bodies. The old dancer was short with big busts and behind and a corset, and all that hair piled up with bird of paradise feathers in it. Now we have stripped the girls almost naked; who wants to see a costume dance? We have taller, better-looking dancers and they are a million times better. The bodies are ready for anything, we use them faster. People now look at the dancers, not a story. Timing is different now and music is no longer an accompaniment.

People criticize me because our dancing is not intellectual, because it doesn't mean anything. Dances are just flowers, and flowers grow without any literal meaning, they are just beautiful.

We are flowers, we just grow, so you can't reject us and say, "You don't mean anything to us, what are you telling us, what's the story? Out!" We just smell nice and we look pink. I have to defend myself because I'm a flower? I won't. They are wrong, not I.

When I stage a ballet (I don't use that word 'create'; God creates and I assemble what already has been created) I try to find interesting proportions of movement in time and space because music is time. It's not the melody that counts, it is the time it gives you. It's up to the choreographer to know what sound represents harmonically, and melodically and rhythmically and then manipulate the gesture into the time and see if it gives any visual pleasure when you look at it. Steps don't exist in themselves, there is no such thing as a ready-made combination. You have to use your legs and hands that are ready to move in any direction at any speed at any time, the maximum the body can do. You can then say you must slow down here, go a little higher there, you should be here at this and that. Lots of things are involved and also the quality of sound and what you think the final music must do, how the sound looks.

I don't think lots, I just manipulate. Finally I have to accept it myself; I am the audience, the judge. If I like it, nobody else can advise me, even the dancers. They are obedient animals. They are trained to wait and wait and wait until you say do this and they do, stop and they stop. You say count to 175 and they will count to 175. Then you can say thank you, now go home. That's all you can do. If they are involved it will be a mess, impossible. Eventually, when the whole thing comes to life, they will understand what it is. But before it does, you cannot improvise; you have to devise, separate, analyze, sift through and slowly feed them and while you're doing it you have to show them every position physically.

Without dancers I cannot do anything. Some choreographers work out all their ballets by dancing themselves in front of a mirror.

Then they write it all down. I don't do that. To me ballet exists only when people are performing, otherwise it doesn't exist. When I use dancers, I want to make things for their bodies to do; their bodies are going to entertain, not mine. My ideas don't exist until their muscles are shown to these people. If I didn't have dancers I like to be with—because I like to look at them and show how they look and move—then I would never think of dance. When I finish rehearsals I forget I ever heard of dance.

That's the difference between some choreographers and myself. Some say, "There doesn't exist in this world a dancer who is good enough to dance what my ideas are. If there was such a dancer he would be the greatest thing in the world." I say just the opposite; I am not good enough. I have beautiful dancers to work with and if I had better ideas they would look even better.

When they dance and make a mistake and know why they were wrong, I don't mind. But when they don't know, *that's* the disaster. As Stravinsky said: "I don't care that they make wrong notes as long as they know they are doing it." Stravinsky taught me a lot: what I am doing now, my approach to time. Through his ideas I improved myself and I listen to everything he says. My friend Nicolas Nabokov and I first started talking about *Don Quixote* 20 years ago. Through the years I would see him and say, "How about doing it?" Then last year we began work. We sat and we talked and we talked and we talked and we sang this and that and then we decided on 30 minutes of this, one hour and a half of this, a minute and a half of that in that tempo that goes faster, plays louder and so on. He started to write, then when sound was actually composed I started to put movement into that music. You can't work out what you want in advance.

Don Quixote, like the 50 other ballets we dance, will never go to the library, it will never be preserved. Only with these people now,

on stage, does it exist. It is not sad at all. It is wonderful, it is now. It is alive. It is like a butterfly. I always say butterflies of yesterday don't exist. But if a butterfly would talk and say, "Remember me from last year? Yes, I'm a little older but I'm still alive," you would be terrified.

I am only interested in these people I am surrounded with, I am working with; these people who are looking at it and these people who are dancing it. I like to live now, today. What will be 10 years from now, 100 years, who cares? One hundred years from now there won't be the ballet as we're doing it today. Just like 100 years ago; you'd laugh if you saw Carlotta Grisi or Taglioni dance today. We have got to enjoy the now.

But I am a teacher, that is my contribution. I learn how to behave on stage, acquire new technique, then go to the schools and teach the children this new technique. This technique is ability, not speed. When I say "technique" people say, "Ah, he is just a mechanical gadget." They call me a mathematician. I have no soul, naturally. But of Mozart they also said, "He is heartless as a bird." I say technique is the ability to have agility and the mechanics to express it.

Dancers come to me and they develop speed and grace and ability and musicality. And they look unfortunately the way I want them to look. I don't take suggestions from dancers because when they come to me they don't know anything and I teach them. The egg cannot tell the chicken how to lay eggs. I lay my own eggs, nobody can tell me how.

I like to do things certain ways and I disagree with everybody but I don't even want to argue. That's what I want and around me it's going to be like that. I'm not old—I've just lived a long time and I'm old enough not to succumb to other people's tastes. Just a few more years and that's all.

Then they can take over.

Significant Balanchine Works

1920 *La Nuit*
1925 *L'Enfant et les sortilèges*
       Le Chant du rossignol
1926 *The Triumph of Neptune*
1927 *La Chatte*
1928 *Apollon Musagète (Apollo)*
1929 *Le Bal*
       The Prodigal Son
1932 *Cotillon*
       La Concurrence
1933 *Mozartiana*
       Les Sept Péchés Capitaux
          (The Seven Deadly Sins)
       L'Errante
1934 *Serenade*
1936 *On Your Toes*
       Orpheus and Eurydice
1937 *Babes in Arms*
       The Card Party
       Le Baiser de la Fée

1938 *I Married an Angel*
       The Boys from Syracuse
       The Goldwyn Follies
1940 *Louisiana Purchase*
       Cabin in the Sky
1941 *Balustrade*
       Ballet Imperial
          (Tchaikovsky Piano
          Concerto No. 2)
       Concerto Barocco
1942 *The Ballet of the Elephants*
1944 *Song of Norway*
       Danses Concertantes
1946 *Night Shadow*
          (La Sonnambula)
       The Four Temperaments
1947 *Le Palais de cristal*
          (Symphony in C)
       Symphonie Concertante
       Theme and Variations

Significant Balanchine Works

1948 *Orpheus*
      Where's Charley?
1949 *Firebird*
      Bourrée Fantasque
1951 *La Valse*
      Swan Lake (Act II)
1952 *Scotch Symphony*
      Metamorphoses
1954 *Opus 34*
      The Nutcracker
      Western Symphony
      Ivesiana
1955 *Pas de Dix*
1956 *Allegro Brillante*
      Divertimento No. 15
1957 *Square Dance*
      Agon
1958 *Gounod Symphony*
      Stars and Stripes
1959 *Episodes*
1960 *Tchaikovsky Pas de Deux*
      Donizetti Variations
      Monumentum pro Gesualdo
      Liebeslieder Walzer
1961 *Raymonda Variations*
1962 *A Midsummer Night's Dream*
1963 *Bugaku*
      *Movements for Piano and
         Orchestra*
      Meditation
1964 *Tarantella*

1965 *Harlequinade*
      Don Quixote
1966 *Brahms–Schoenberg Quartet*
1967 *Jewels*
1968 *Slaughter on Tenth Avenue*
      La Source
1970 *Who Cares?*
      Tchaikovsky Suite No. 3
1972 *Symphony in Three
         Movements*
      Stravinsky Violin Concerto
      Duo Concertant
1973 *Cortège Hongrois*
1974 *Variations pour une Porte et
         un Soupir*
      Coppélia (with Alexandra
         Danilova)
1975 *Sonatine*
      Le Tombeau de Couperin
      Tzigane
      The Steadfast Tin Soldier
1976 *Chaconne*
      Union Jack
1977 *Vienna Waltzes*
1978 *Ballo della Regina*
      Kammermusik No. 2
1980 *Ballade*
      Walpurgisnacht Ballet
      *Robert Schumann's
         "Davidsbündlertänze"*
1981 *Mozartiana*

Sources

There is an extraordinarily large Balanchine bibliography, beginning with two large-scale biographies. The earlier was *Balanchine: A Biography*, by Bernard Taper (Harper & Row, 1963; later editions, Macmillan and Times Books)—essential, as well as highly readable. It began as a *New Yorker* profile, which is why it has such immediacy and verisimilitude. Balanchine was extremely forthcoming with Taper, as were colleagues and friends—reading Taper, you feel, as you do with all classic *New Yorker* profiles, that you're listening in on the subject. Balanchine's being profiled in the magazine was a major event for New York City Ballet in those days when audiences were by no means guaranteed. The positive results of *The New Yorker*'s publication led Balanchine to agree to cooperate with Taper on the expanded version of the profile that became the book. It was later twice updated, the second time in 1984 just after Balanchine's death, and it remains a basic source.

Richard Buckle's *George Balanchine: Ballet Master* (Random House, 1988) was written in collaboration with John Taras, a long-time associate of Balanchine's. Because Buckle was a leading British dance critic and Taras was so intimately involved in the Balanchine enterprise, their book is by definition more knowledgeable about ballet than Taper's, and they had available to them previously un-

published personal recollections and letters. They also were writing five years after Balanchine's death. As a result, their book has interesting new things to tell us, although it lacks Taper's immediacy. The two biographies complement each other.

There is also an interesting take on Balanchine in a shorter but shrewd biography, *Balletmaster: A Dancer's View of Balanchine,* by the English ballerina (and star of *The Red Shoes*) Moira Shearer (Putnam, 1987). In 1950 Shearer was one of the dancers to whom Balanchine taught *Ballet Imperial* when he set it on London's Royal Ballet. He very much liked her dancing, and to a greater degree than most English dancers of her day, she very much admired his work.

Two other books are vital to understanding Balanchine. One is *I Remember Balanchine,* edited by Francis Mason (Doubleday, 1991), in which eighty-five of Balanchine's dancers, colleagues, friends— and wives—recall him. It includes the crucial long article by Yuri Slonimsky that had originally appeared in *Ballet Review* in 1976— the single most important source for Balanchine's early years. Also valuable are the memories of Tamara Geva, Alexandra Danilova, and Maria Tallchief, of Marie-Jeanne and Ray Bolger, of Tamara Toumanova and Ruthanna Boris, of Peter Martins and Edward Villella, of Lincoln Kirstein; indeed, of all the contributors.

And then there is Solomon Volkov's *Balanchine's Tchaikovsky* (Simon & Schuster, 1985), a book of interviews that Volkov conducted at the very end of Balanchine's life. Centered on his views about Tchaikovsky, it ranges over many aspects of Balanchine's history, and is highly emotional at times. Clearly, Balanchine felt at home with Volkov, a musician and fellow-Petersburgian, and talking about Tchaikovsky triggered memories and feelings that in his old age he was prepared to share.

Another book of interviews—Robert Tracy's *Balanchine's Balleri-*

nas (Linden Press/Simon & Schuster, 1983)—is another fascinating source of information, covering as it does the entire gamut of Balanchine's muses, from Danilova, Geva, and Doubrovska through Mary Ellen Moylan, Maria Tallchief, Diana Adams, Allegra Kent, and Violette Verdy to Suzanne Farrell, Karin von Aroldingen, and Darci Kistler.

There are two basic books about the Balanchine repertory: the magnificent *Choreography by George Balanchine: A Catalogue of Works* (Eakins Press Foundation, 1983), prepared by the dedicated team of Leslie George Katz, Nancy Lassalle, Harvey Simmonds, and Nancy Reynolds, a labor of love without which we would be sadly ignorant of the scope and details of Balanchine's achievement; and Nancy Reynolds's *Repertory in Review* (Dial Press, 1977), an invaluable book on the repertory of New York City Ballet, which provides not only important data but a brilliantly chosen and edited gathering of critical comment on all the company's ballets up to that time.

The two great dance critics who have tracked Balanchine's achievement are Edwin Denby and Arlene Croce. The latest collections of their work are Denby's *Dance Writings and Poetry* (Yale University Press, 1998) and Croce's *Writing in the Dark, Dancing in The New Yorker* (Farrar, Straus & Giroux, 2000), both assembled and edited by Robert Cornfield. These are essential books in the Balanchine literature. Equally compelling is the long essay on Balanchine's art that Croce wrote for *The International Encyclopedia of Dance* (Oxford University Press, 1998).

Many other critics have written tellingly about Balanchine, from New York's daily reviewers, beginning with John Martin in the *New York Times* and Walter Terry in the *New York Herald Tribune,* to important weekly critics, in particular Joan Acocella, Nancy Goldner, Robert Greskovic, and Tobi Tobias. B. H. Haggin's *Ballet Chronicle* (Horizon, 1970) provides a fascinating running commentary on

Balanchine's work. Another stimulating approach is to be found in Robert Garis's *Following Balanchine* (Yale University Press, 1997). The most acute criticism from England is to be found in Richard Buckle's *The Adventures of a Ballet Critic* (Cresset, 1953).

And of course there are the voluminous writings of Lincoln Kirstein, that tireless and brilliant enthusiast, polemicist, and critic. For the purposes of this book I have drawn mostly on *By With To & From: A Lincoln Kirstein Reader*, edited by Nicholas Jenkins (Farrar, Straus & Giroux, 1991); on a long seminal essay that is contained in Nancy Reynolds's *Repertory in Review*; and on the text of *The New York City Ballet* (Alfred A. Knopf, 1973), which was later expanded into *Thirty Years* (Alfred A. Knopf, 1978) and of which I was the editor.

I was also the editor of *Suki Schorer on Balanchine Technique* (Alfred A. Knopf, 1999), a remarkable anatomization of what Balanchine demanded from the dancers and teachers at the School of American Ballet. To the extent that Balanchine's ideas on dance technique can be codified, Schorer has done it—with the help of countless anecdotes and memories of Balanchine in the studio.

There are many memoirs by former Balanchine dancers, and all of them add to the general picture we have of him as man and choreographer. Four of his wives have written autobiographies: Tamara Geva's *Split Seconds* (Harper & Row, 1972); Alexandra Danilova's *Choura* (Alfred A. Knopf, 1986); Vera Zorina's *Zorina* (Farrar, Straus & Giroux, 1986); and Maria Tallchief's *Maria Tallchief: America's Prima Ballerina* (Henry Holt, 1997). There are also fascinating accounts of his life and work by Allegra Kent (*Once a Dancer . . .* ; St. Martin's, 1997), Suzanne Farrell (*Holding On to the Air*; Summit, 1990), Merrill Ashley (*Dancing for Balanchine*; Dutton, 1984), Edward Villella (*Prodigal Son*; Simon & Schuster, 1992), and Peter Martins (*Far from Denmark*; Little, Brown, 1982).

Remembering Mr. B, a loving collection of reminiscences and tributes by his dancers, was assembled and privately printed by Karin von Aroldingen to commemorate his one hundredth birthday in 2004.

Balanchine figures, if less prominently, in the memoirs of Lydia Sokolova, Alice Nikitina, Marie Rambert, Ninette de Valois, Paul Taylor, Nathan Milstein, Vernon Duke; in *Speaking of Diaghilev*, a series of interviews compiled by John Drummond; in the writings of Virgil Thomson and Agnes de Mille; in the collected criticism of André Levinson.

Several dance histories track Balanchine's career through important periods of his life. *Soviet Choreographers in the 1920s* by Elizabeth Souritz (Duke University Press, 1990) places him in the context of Soviet dance before his departure in 1924; Lynn Garafola's *Diaghilev's Ballets Russes* (Oxford University Press, 1989) provides important background for the Diaghilev period. A particularly fascinating running account of the Diaghilev association appears in the *The Diaghilev Ballet 1909–1929* (Constable, 1953), the memoirs of S. L. Grigoriev, who was Diaghilev's right-hand man from the beginning to the end. Kathrine Sorley Walker's *De Basil's Ballets Russes* (Atheneum, 1983) is the authority on Balanchine's association with that company; Jack Anderson's *The One and Only: The Ballet Russe de Monte Carlo* (Princeton Book Co., 1981) is instructive on the Monte Carlo period of his life; Anatole Chujoy's *The New York City Ballet* (Alfred A. Knopf, 1954) has much to say. And Robert Maiorano and Valerie Brooks's *Balanchine's Mozartiana: The Making of a Masterpiece* (Freundlich Books, 1985) is a unique chronicle of the creation of a single ballet, written by a former City Ballet dancer.

Charles M. Joseph's *Stravinsky & Balanchine* (Yale University Press, 2002) is the most comprehensive and insightful investigation into the artistic relationship between the two men, and of course

Robert Craft, both as a critic and as Stravinsky's collaborator and scribe, is a major commentator on Balanchine's art.

Countless articles on Balanchine have appeared in scholarly publications and journals. Two important sources: *Dance Index,* which Lincoln Kirstein began in 1946, and *Ballet Review,* which Arlene Croce founded and which has since been edited by Robert Cornfield and Francis Mason. A long, illuminating conversation between Balanchine and W. McNeil Lowry appeared in *The New Yorker* in 1983. And there is *Balanchine's Complete Stories of the Great Ballets,* written with Francis Mason (Doubleday, 1954).

An essential complement to all the written testimony about Balanchine is the superb two-hour documentary *Balanchine,* made for the PBS series *Dance in America* shortly after his death, and now available on VHS and DVD.

Finally, we must be grateful to the many photographers who have recorded Balanchine and his art so lovingly. They include George Platt Lynes, Fred Fehl, Martha Swope, Paul Kolnik, and Costas.

Acknowledgments

Barbara Horgan, for many years Balanchine's personal assistant and, after his death, the head of the Balanchine Trust and the Balanchine Foundation, has been a constant source of information, sympathy, and patience. Everyone who cares about Balanchine owes her an immense debt of gratitude.

Other people who have generously given me their time include Andrei Balanchivadze, Vida Brown, Frederic Franklin, Beth Genné, Elizabeth Kendall, Nancy Lassalle, Francis Mason, Maria Tallchief, the late John Taras, and Karin von Aroldingen. I am especially grateful to Ruthanna Boris, John Clifford, and Barbara Milberg, who have all allowed me to quote from as-yet-unpublished memoirs. Through the years I have talked endlessly about Balanchine with Allegra Kent, Suki Schorer, and Edward Villella. And I attended countless performances of City Ballet with Lincoln Kirstein and Arlene Croce, from both of whom I learned so much.

I'm particularly indebted to Joan Accocella, Adam Begley, Robert Cornfield, Allegra Kent, Chip McGrath, Alastair Macaulay, and Richard Overstreet for reading the manuscript and helping me improve it. And I must also thank the Dance Collection at the Performing Arts Library at Lincoln Center—especially Madeleine

215

Acknowledgments

Nichols and Monica Moseley—and the New York City Ballet archive, managed by Heather Heckman, as well as Lydia Harmson at City Ballet, for helping with the photographs. I want to thank Graydon Carter (and *Vanity Fair*) for permitting me to cannibalize a long article, "Six Ways of Looking at the New York City Ballet," that I wrote for the magazine in 1998 to celebrate the company's fiftieth anniversary.

And of course I am grateful to James Atlas for commissioning this book and seeing it through publication; to his endlessly helpful assistant, Lauren Zeranski; to my highly knowledgeable and very sympathetic copyeditor, Sue Llewellyn; to my infinitely patient (and talented) designer, Amy Hill; and to Roni Axelrod, that rare production director who knows how to bend the rules.

. . .

Photographs on pages 6 (*top left and right*) 28, 54, 55, 86, 87, 115, 162, and 184 (*top left*), courtesy of the New York City Ballet Archive, Ballet Society; pages 29, 73, 183, 184 (*bottom*), and 185, courtesy of the Jerome Robbins Dance Division, The New York Public Library for the Performing Arts, Astor, Lenox and Tilden Foundations; pages 72, 116, and 147, courtesy of Martha Swope; page 114 (*top*), courtesy of New York City Ballet Archive, Tanaquil LeClercq Collection; page 114 (*bottom*), by Gordon Parks/TimeLife Pictures/Getty Images; page 146, copyright Ray Schorr; page 174 (*top*), courtesy of Costas; page 174 (*bottom*), courtesy of Paul Kolnik; title page and page 184 (*top right*), copyright George Platt Lynes.